THE SMOKE OF DISTANT FIRES

T0272952

THE SMOKE OF DISTANT FIRES

POEMS

EDUARDO CHIRINOS

TRANSLATED FROM THE SPANISH BY G. J. RACZ
INTRODUCTION BY DANIEL SHAPIRO

OPEN LETTER
LITERARY TRANSLATIONS FROM THE UNIVERSITY OF ROCHESTER

ACKNOWLEDGEMENTS

Some of the translations in this volume have been published before, in slightly different form, in the following venues:

Borderlands: Texas Poetry Review: "Love Poem with Dark Face"; *Cincinnati Review*: "Athanasius and the Ark or the Conversion of Saint Eustace," "Thirteen Winters with Snow," "The Smoke of Distant Fires"; *Literal, Latin American Voices*: "Notes for a Confession with Rutabagas"; *Reasons for Writing Poetry* (Salt Publishing, 2011): "A Theory of Sight After a Poem by Seferis," "The Book of My Life or My Conversations with Saint Teresa of Ávila," "Putting My Library in Order Before Bedtime," "Letters that Arrive without Fanfare."

.

Library of Congress Cataloging-in-Publication Data:

Chirinos Arrieta, Eduardo, 1960-
    [Humo de incendios lejanos. English & Spanish]
    The smoke of distant fires : poems / by Eduardo Chirinos ; translated from
the Spanish by G.J. Racz ; introduction by Daniel Shapiro. — 1st ed.
      p. cm.
    Includes bibliographical references.
    Text in English and Spanish.
    ISBN-13: 978-1-934824-38-2 (pbk. : alk. paper)
    ISBN-10: 1-934824-38-0 (pbk. : alk. paper)
  1. Chirinos Arrieta, Eduardo, 1960- — Translations into English.
  I. Racz, Gregory Joseph. II. Title.
    PQ8498.13.H54H8613 2011
    861'.64—dc23

                  2011027622

Printed on acid-free paper in the United States of America.

Text set in Chaparral.

Design by N. J. Furl

Open Letter is the University of Rochester's nonprofit, literary translation press:
Lattimore Hall 411, Box 270082, Rochester, NY 14627

www.openletterbooks.org

For Jannine, who came up with the title.

CONTENTS

INTRODUCTION:
IMAGE, VOICE, AND MUSIC
IN *THE SMOKE OF DISTANT FIRES*

I first had the opportunity to meet Eduardo Chirinos and read his poetry in 1997, when I presented him along with various other Peruvian writers in a special program at the Americas Society in New York. The program complemented a Peruvian issue of the Society's publication, *Review: Literature and Arts of the Americas*, which showcased poetry, fiction, and essays by the participating writers.[1]

At the time, I was struck by Chirinos's whimsical language, the lightness of touch in his poems, their exploration of the life of the imagination. One poem in particular, "The Bayard Street Tightrope Walker," stayed with me. The poem opens as follows: "He proceeds on tippy-toes, the Bayard Street Tightrope Walker, / his gaze avoiding the abyss as he rips all pretension out by the roots."[2] This poem seemed like an apt metaphor for this particular poet—and for poets in general—a kind of unassuming everyman who possesses an aerial

---

1. "Writing Today in Peru," Americas Society, November 1997. With the collaboration of the Latin American Writers Institute/CUNY. *Review: Latin American Literature and Arts*, no. 57, Fall 1998.

2. "The Bayard Street Tightrope Walker," trans. G.J. Racz. In *Reasons for Writing Poetry* (London: Salt Publishing, 2011).

perspective on the world, his act of suspension and balance suggesting worlds "lighter than air."

Since those initial encounters, I've read other works of Chirinos—he is the author of sixteen poetry collections as well as literary criticism and children's literature—and have enjoyed watching, largely retroactively, his development as a poet, from the early *Cuadernos de Horacio Morell* (1981; Notebooks of Horacio Morell) to *Escrito en Missoula* (2003; *Written in Missoula*, 2011), among other books of poems. His body of work thus far displays a rich canvas—one populated with numerous personas and delightful images—and underscores a deep feeling for place, from his native Peru to Montana, where he now lives and teaches. In his published collections to date, his poetic voice demonstrates a sense of authority; his language exudes lyricism and music; and the poems explore themes relating to desire, the creative impulse, and loss in its various manifestations.

And now we have *Humo de incendios lejanos* (2009), translated as *The Smoke of Distant Fires* by G. J. Racz, whose seamless English version perfectly reflects the vivid language and singular voice as well as the animated spirit and cohesive wholeness of the original text. The translation reads, as it should, as if it were written in English. The book culminates the poet's oeuvre to date, demonstrating, as I see it, a movement from image to voice, from collections of individual poems to a sustained long poem, from the fragmentary utterings of his first persona, "Horacio Morell"—whom the author describes in that book's fictional prologue as "a marginal writer"—to a multidimensional *arte poética* in which the voice of the author's alter ego, "Eduardo," interacts with a panoply of speakers.

First, a look at the scope and organization of the collection. As suggested, the work is a book-length text, a meditation that's structured as a series of thirteen poems, each divided into ten parts of varying line-lengths; each poem is inspired by a line of verse or a work of art by poets and artists including John Ashbery, Robert

Frost, Emily Dickinson, Juan Larrea, Édouard Manet, and St. Teresa of Ávila. The poems bear evocative titles such as "Love Poem With Dark Face," "Notes for a Confession with Rutagabas," "Thirteen Winters with Snow," "What the Birdsong Says," and, of course, "The Smoke of Distant Fires."

The language and imagery run the gamut, from the experiential to the metaphysical, from the whimsical to the allegorical, from striking images that occur only once to those that recur throughout the collection. Among the latter group is the repeating series, "a bonfire, a fistful of snow . . . a freshly cut rose," which functions like an informal refrain, providing emotional and metaphorical resonance. Some of the images elsewhere suggest fables by Aesop or Kipling. One of my favorites concerns fantastic beasts including the "tragelaph," "the offspring of a billy goat and doe" (p. 55). All in all, this is an erudite poetry, packed with allusions to a wide breadth of literature, including the classics—Romulus and Remus, the Sphinx, Ganymede, the Sirens, and Helen of Troy all make an appearance here. It's also a work sprinkled with images from popular culture, such as Popeye and Batman and, at the other end of the spectrum, swans, larks, and angels, those messengers of the sublime.

Then there's the movement of language in the collection and its relationship to voice. The poetry veritably explodes from line to line, propelling itself from section to section, as if racing to its conclusion. Ambiguous syntax serves this momentum, also encouraging thematic ambiguity. Most importantly, I believe, this movement is reinforced by the book's voice, because this is a book dominated by voice—one that's assertive yet questioning—as well as by the free-floating consciousness it represents. Unlike much contemporary poetry, there is very little silence in these poems—they possess a frenetic quality, almost like incessant speech. The poem rushes onward from beginning to end, ranging far and wide over the terrain of the imagination. "[You] talk so much about yourself you'll end up being another person" (p. 91), one speaker states. Reflecting that plurality, the overall voice recalls poets as varied and idiosyncratic as Whitman, Rilke, and Milosz, as well as more contemporary ones, including Norman Dubie, an innovative creator of personas; the quirky and conversational Russell Edson; and Vasko Popa, author of the "little box" poems.

If we shift from form to meaning, we may describe *The Smoke of Distant Fires* as a work of meta-poetry; that is, in addition to all its allusions, references, and affinities with other voices, it is self-referential. To my mind, its most all-encompassing theme is what constitutes the creative process: it is poetry about writing poetry. This is explored in its various facets throughout the collection.

Thus the first poem, "Love Poem with Dark Face," is a kind of invocation, initiating the search for a title and the reason for creating the poem. It's here where the concept of the muse is also introduced: she first appears in an art gallery, "a woman with sad eyes devours rats devours picassos" (p. 11), making other appearances in different guises. This poem also touches on the enigmatic quality of poetry in general, echoed in its title and epigraph, a line by Yves Bonnefoy: "I will hold in my hands your dark face" (p. 11).

The poems that follow address different elements of the poetic experience: the role of mystery in poetry, as explored in the image of an octopus ("A Theory of Sight After a Poem by Seferis"); the realm of fantasy as suggested by rutabagas ("Notes for a Confession with Rutabagas"); the mystical dimension of poetry ("The Book of My Life or My Conversations with Saint Teresa of Ávila"); the figure of the solitary writer in his room ("Fable of the Lark and the Moon"); and poetry's visual aspect as in a painting by Manet ("Flowers and Flies for Berthe Morisot"). Successive poems deal with voice, music, and silence ("Putting My Library in Order Before Bedtime"); "the blankness of the page" à la Robert Frost ("Thirteen Winters with Snow"); poetry as enigma, exemplified by Emily Dickinson's cryptic word-games ("Exercises for Blocking Out the Rain"); and the enigma par excellence, represented by the image of the Sphinx ("Letters that Arrive without Fanfare").

In the final poem, the speaker ponders, "I wonder where the title the smoke of distant fires comes from," bringing the poem full-circle, recalling other images that have appeared—including heliotropes and blue begonias, a dog barking at the moon, and the serpent of Lucifer—concluding, aptly, that "the metaphor / is burning" (p. 101).

As stated earlier, I believe that this book represents a progression in Chirinos's work from image to voice; perhaps I should go further and say "from image to music." A pivotal point along that trajectory would be his *Breve historia de la música* (2001; A Brief History of Music), whose poems take pieces such as the *Brandenburg Concertos*, *Für Elise*, and *The Four Seasons* as leaping-off points for jewel-like conceits. Like music, the lines are broken up from page to page, together embodying a book-length work bound by a sustained voice. As in the earlier collection, but even more so here, music holds the key to understanding *The Smoke of Distant Fires*—its organization, its lyricism, its deep resonance as poetry, as well as its disembodied nature, its pure abstraction. Peruvian critic José Miguel Oviedo has called the parts within each poem "variations" or "suites."[3] And, as the speaker anticipates nearly halfway through the book, "you have the music can you wait for the words?" (p. 65)

The poetic voice soars over time and space, now unmoored from any one place, situation or character; the collective poem possesses absolute freedom. This freedom applies even to the collection's title, stated on the title-page and in the poem's closing lines. The work concludes ambiguously, on a note that leaves the poem and the book open-ended. That closing line is presented offhandedly, almost off-stage (I thought of Dickinson's presentation of Death in "I Heard a Fly

---

3. Source: http://www.letraslibres.com/index.php?art=14117

Buzz When I Died")—undercutting the reader's expectations with a final surprise.

Complex and multidimensional, *The Smoke of Distant Fires* encompasses a wholeness of vision, one that's expansive, even symphonic. Anticipating further poetic encounters, I can only applaud Eduardo Chirinos and G. J. Racz for this singular feat.

Daniel Shapiro
April 2011

THE SMOKE OF DISTANT FIRES

POEMA DE AMOR CON ROSTRO OSCURO

J'aurai dans mes mains ton visage obscur
—Yves Bonnefoy

[1]
cómo llamar este poema lo llamaré fluir de aposentos
lo llamaré estrépito de frondas poema de amor con rostro
oscuro hermoso título alguien no sé quién me dice cuídate
de los significados no busques verdad detrás de la belleza
aprende a respirar con la mirada en una galería de arte
una mujer de ojos tristes devora ratas devora picassos
duerme en cuartos de hospital escucha esta historia érase
una vez una princesa bah la muerte no tardará en aparecer
la muerte sus ojos azules sobre mi plato vacío

[2]
nunca sabrá quién soy es ciega y aborrece las miradas
le ofrezco una hoguera un puñado de nieve le ofrezco
una rosa cortada ¿ahora de qué hablamos? hablemos
del cielo hablemos del miedo esta noche habrá tormenta
mejor caer y nunca levantarse cómo le pregunto
y desaparece no sé si volverá sin embargo espero
con mi diente de leche con mi vieja colección
de estampillas con mi hoja de afeitar y un espejo
de noche viene me susurra al oído eres único me dice
en un millón de años sabré su verdadero nombre
su rostro oscuro pleno de cielo pleno de miedo

LOVE POEM WITH DARK FACE

J'aurais dans mes mains ton visage obscur
—Yves Bonnefoy

[1]
what should i call this poem i'll call it a rush of chambers
a racket of foliage i'll call it love poem with dark
face pretty title someone i don't know who tells me watch
out for words with meaning don't look for truth in beauty
learn to breathe with your gaze in an art gallery
a woman with sad eyes devours rats devours picassos
sleeps in hospital rooms listen to this story once upon
a time a princess bah death will not be long in coming
death with its blue eyes on my empty plate

[2]
she'll never know who i am she's blind and hates when people
look at her i offer her a bonfire a fistful of snow offer her
a freshly cut rose what should we talk about now? let's talk
about the sky let's talk about fear there's going to be a storm tonight
a person would do better to drop and never get up how's that i ask
but she disappears i don't know if she'll ever return still
i wait with my milk tooth with my old stamp
collection with my razor blade and a mirror at night
she comes whispers in my ear there's no one but you
in a million years i'll learn her real name know
her dark face flush with sky flush with fear

[3]

¿por qué escribo esto? pupila incandescente soy un cisne
sueño morir en tu sueño en una caja donde arda el infierno
donde todo enceguezca la tormenta nada dice es muda
debiste haberme mirado aquella vez los viñedos
florecían las vacas pastaban yo era feliz tú eras feliz
la transparencia del enigma entibiaba el café la disección
del mito la muerte de cualquier teoría soy un cisne
mi sueño es morir en tu sueño ¿por qué no me miraste?

[4]

los estudiantes preguntaron el significado del dolor
con una hoja de afeitar le corté el dedo a una muñeca
no hubo sangre no hubo parpadeo dije esto es el dolor

[5]

simultáneamente leo y escribo es lo justo las montañas
aprueban por exceso la noche cierra un ojo con el otro
me contempla no hay nada alrededor hay flores de plástico
purgatorios a punto de cerrarse y puertas y ventanas la luz
se impacienta el tiempo destruye los relojes ¿puedo hablar?
no es necesario las páginas arden tu lámpara se quema
yo me desnudo dejo que el frío encienda mi pene

[6]

ahora arribo a la parte más difícil del relato
a la parte donde hablo de marsopas y delfines la mujer
de ojos tristes vomita ratas en el excusado yo hablo
de mi deseo no quiero que lo sepa diré sólo una palabra
rozaré apenas su cabello y si huye ah las palabras perdidas
las habitaciones oscuras cada cual con su estertor de pájaros
cada cual remontando su vuelo la mujer cierra los ojos

[3]

why am i writing this? you incandescent pupil i'm a swan
that dreams of dying in your dream inside a box where hell burns
where everything is blinding the storm doesn't say a word stays mute
you should have seen me that time the vineyards were
in bloom the cows were grazing i was happy you were happy
the enigma's transparence cooled our coffee the myth's
dissection the death of any and all theories i'm a swan
my dream is to die in your dream why didn't you look at me?

[4]

my students asked me what is the meaning of pain
so i sliced a doll's finger with a razor blade there
was no blood no batting of lashes this i told them is pain

[5]

i read and write at the same time it's only proper the mountains
overwhelmingly approve the night shuts one eye and looks at me
with the other there is nothing around but plastic flowers
purgatories on the brink of closure doors and windows the light
grows impatient time destroys clocks may i speak?
there's no need to the pages are on fire your lamp is burning
i take off my clothes and let the cold ignite my penis

[6]

now i come to the hardest part of the story the part
where i talk about porpoises and dolphins the woman
with the sad eyes vomits rats into the toilet i speak of
my desire i don't want her to know about it i'll just say a word
brush my hand against her hair and if she runs ah the lost words
the dark rooms each with its death rattle of birds
all soaring skyward the woman closes her eyes

penétrame dice he olvidado tu nombre no tengo
ningún nombre de lo más alto de la cama un dios observa
su cuerpo herido me dice cuánto me desea

[7]
sombrío ven cuando quieras arderé en tu memoria quemaré
tu lengua cualquier desorden tendrá cabida en tus sentidos
cualquier gesto alegoría en nuestras manos tengo para ti
un cuaderno un vaso de agua peces muertos le dije sombría
adoro los cuadernos espero cada noche un vaso de agua
en mi lengua peces muertos son delirio los estudiantes
preguntan qué es delirio me abro la camisa y les muestro
tus senos esto es delirio

[8]
fluir de aposentos desbordados es hora de jugar tú eres
sombra yo soy luz tú lames mis heridas yo me hundo
en el relámpago en las dos oscuridades donde duermes
donde espero la palabra humo es la palabra mañana
tu cuerpo y mi cuerpo cantarán y habrá otra vez un bosque
desplegándose a mis ojos una persiana abierta un manantial
de ángeles sobre la ropa sucia cuéntame algo cualquier cosa
lo importante es despertar y no ceder al sueño se pudren
los amores felices se pudren los amores desgraciados
adiós me dice adiós hay heridas y flores en sus manos

[9]
dejar vagar el cuerpo no el amor en otros cuerpos
así comienza el exilio la expulsión violenta una luz
muy hermosa agoniza en los escombros nadie puede verlo
el hielo es engañoso cuando brilla el cielo un pasado
irrevocable una voz que lastima una voz que no llega

go in me she says i've forgotten your name i don't have
a name from high above the bed a god observes us
his wounded body conveying how much she wants me

[7]
sorrowful boy come whenever you like i'll burn in your memory sear
your tongue all kinds of confusion will find a place in your senses
any expression will be allegory in our hands i have a notebook
for you a glass of water some dead fish i said to her sorrowful girl
i love notebooks await every night a glass of water
on my tongue dead fish are a delirium my students
ask what's delirium i unbutton my shirt and show them
your breasts this is delirium

[8]
a rush of overflowing chambers it's playtime now you're
the shadow and i'm the light you lick my wounds while i sink
into the lightning flash into both sets of darkness where you sleep
and i await the word smoke is the word tomorrow
your body and mine will sing and there will again be woods
unfurling before my eyes open venetian blinds a fount
of angels atop the dirty laundry tell me a story anything
what's important is that we awaken and not give in to sleep
happy loves rot as surely as blighted ones do
bye bye she says bye bye flowers in her wounded hands

[9]
to let the body not love drift through other bodies
that's how banishment how violent expulsion begins quite
a lovely light is dying amid the debris no one can see it
ice is deceptive when it shines bright the sky an irrevocable
past a voice inspiring pity a voice that never reaches us

[10]

inquieta la geometría del mármol bajo sus pies
la metáfora buscada es un ciclón azul la callecita oscura
la tumba de cualquier proyecto aunque nada lo impida
podemos ser felices pero aquí no hay nadie sólo yo
y las palabras los viajes a destiempo los buses escarlata
su luz recuerdo oscurecía el dolor y sin embargo se fue
la seguí hasta perderla nadie me enseñó a perder un deseo
nube violeta cubre mi cuerpo los estudiantes preguntan
qué es un cuerpo dibujo en el aire una palabra la palabra
estalla y cae al suelo les digo esto es un cuerpo

[10]
disturbing the marble slab's geometry beneath her feet
the sought-after metaphor is a blue cyclone the dark alley
the grave of all projects though nothing stands in our way
we can be happy but there's no one here only me besides
the words the untimely trips and scarlet buses i remember
her light which made the pain grow dark and still she went away
i followed until i lost her trace no one ever taught me to lose a desire
a purple cloud envelopes my body the students ask me
what is a body i draw a word in the air the word bursts
and drops to the ground this i tell them is a body

TEORÍA DE LA VISIÓN AL PIE DE UN POEMA DE SEFERIS

Θερινὸ ἡλιοστάσι, ΙΑ'

[1]
yo te miraba con toda la luz y oscuridad que poseo así
termina un poema así comienza otro ¿o es acaso el mismo?
nunca estuve en grecia nunca respiré la brisa de los pinos
el monstruo ha muerto su hedor inunda las playas su luz
trae otros cielos otros mares igualmente azules ese mar
está muy lejos cubre de ceniza esta página oscurece mi boca

[2]
mirar sin luz es un arte lo aprendí de niño cerraba
los ojos hasta hacerlos doler hasta olvidarme de mí
qué hermoso decía la dama de negro la dama de blanco
me sentaba en sus rodillas tapaba en silencio mis orejas
me enseñaba a leer decía el exceso de luz oscurece
cuídate del brillo cuando escribas solo y sin luz

[3]
el poema habla de otra cosa habla del mar que dicen
calma del final de una isla muy hermosa de la brisa
cálida deslizándose en tu piel habla de un pulpo
arponeado en los bajíos de su tinta oscureciendo
el agua de la eternidad que precede a la belleza

[4]
compartimos el pan y la sal compartimos el hacha
que partió el árbol compartimos la mesa las flores

A THEORY OF SIGHT AFTER
A POEM BY SEFERIS

Θερινὸ ἡλιοστάσι, ΙΑ´

[1]
i looked at you with all the light and the darkness i possess so
ends one poem and begins another or is it perhaps the same one?
i've never been to greece never breathed in the breeze off the pine trees
the monster is dead its stench overwhelms the beaches its light
brings with it other skies other equally blue seas yet that sea
is very far away it covers this page with ash and darkens my mouth

[2]
looking absent light is an art i learned as a child i would squeeze
my eyes shut until they hurt until i forgot who i was how
lovely the woman in black would say while the woman in white
would sit me on her knees cover my ears so i couldn't hear
and teach me to read too much light can darken things she'd say
be careful of the brightness when you're writing alone absent light

[3]
the poem speaks of something else it speaks of the sea they call
tranquil of how far down a beautiful island goes of the warm
breeze gliding over your skin of an octopus
speared in the shallow sea of its ink darkening
the water of eternity that precedes beauty

[4]
we share bread and salt we share the ax
that chopped down the tree share the table the flowers

la música que escuchamos al dormir es la misma
al despertar nuestro monte no es de egina los pinos
se adormecen ¿cómo he de mirarte?

[5]
la dama de negro dijo antiguamente se creía
que la luz eran rayos que brotaban de los ojos ver
era nombrar el mundo despejar su tiniebla la dama
de blanco dijo antiguamente se creía que la luz
borraba el contorno de las cosas las volvía claras
hasta desaparecer le pregunté cómo era posible
me dijo escribes poemas ¿acaso no lo sabes?

[6]
¿alguna vez escalaré el monte danzaré junto a los pinos
sentiré en mi boca el sabor amargo de la sal alguna vez

veré la tinta del pulpo resollando en la espuma
la luz de este poema oscureciendo el mar?

[7]
no dijo la dama de blanco tu deber es escribir haya
o no haya sol tocar el revés de la cartografía hundirte
en la tinta del pulpo y mirar si es posible mirar pero
no ver sí dijo la dama de negro tu deber es callar haya
o no haya sol torcer hacia dentro la lengua aceptar
el placer y no escribir si es posible no escribir

the music we listen to falling asleep is the same we hear
upon waking our mountain is not from aegina the pines
grow drowsy how should i look at you?

[5]
the woman in black said in olden days people believed
light to be rays that shot forth from eyes seeing meant
naming the world shunting aside its darkness the woman
in white said in olden days people believed light
blurred the outlines of objects making them transparent
until they became invisible i asked her how that was possible
she said you write poems how is it you don't know?

[6]
will i ever scale that mountain dance beside the pine
trees feel the bitter taste of that salt in my mouth

see the octopus's ink panting in the foam
or the light of this poem darkening the sea?

[7]
no the woman in white said your duty is to write whether
or not the sun shines to touch the back of mapmaking to submerge
yourself in the octopus's ink and look if that's possible look but
not see yes the woman in black said your duty is to remain silent
    whether
or not the sun shines to twist your tongue inside your mouth to
    embrace
pleasure and not to write if that's possible not to write

[8]

he abierto el libro en el solsticio de verano
sus páginas me devuelven una voz que no es la mía
esa voz sabe de mí con familiaridad enumera uno
por uno mis defectos la interrogo es inútil esa voz
conserva un mechón de cabellos amarillos la prenda
de un amor imposible el concierto de tchaikovsky
la hora exacta de la muerte de mi abuelo páginas
enteras que había borrado y escrito le dije tú ganas
¿qué quieres de mí?

[9]

hay rayos que parten del sol rayos que parten del ojo
ellos crean las cosas al tocarlas si duermes desaparece
el mundo si despiertas se hunde por el sumidero adónde
va no lo sé pregúntale a leonardo a paracelso pregúntale
el ojo es una geometría de círculos un planeta que gira
sin importarle nada sin detenerse a contemplar el sol qué
turbio el sol cubre de ceniza esta página oscurece mi boca

[10]

siempre lo mismo el mar azul el polvo de egina la tinta
del pulpo encharcada en la voz o en el papel siempre
lo mismo aunque la escena cambie de sueño o de deseo
aunque la belleza diga no y la verdad cierre sus ojos

yo te miro con toda la luz y oscuridad que poseo

[8]

i've opened the book in the summer solstice
its pages give me back a voice that's not mine
yet knows intimate things about me listing my
defects one by one i question it to no avail that voice
preserves within it a lock of blonde hair the token
of a forbidden love a concerto by tchaikovsky
the precise time of my grandfather's death whole
pages i had erased and written i said to it you win
what do you want from me?

[9]

some rays come from the sun some from the eye
creating objects by touching them when you sleep the world
disappears when you wake it sinks into the cesspool where
it goes i couldn't tell you ask leonardo ask paracelsus ask him
the eye is a geometry of circles a planet that spins around
without a care without stopping to observe the sun how turbid
the sun looks covering this page with ash darkening my mouth

[10]

they're always the same the blue sea aegina's dust the octopus's
ink leaving a puddle in one's voice or on the sheet of paper always
the same though the scene change the dream or desire
though beauty say no and truth shut its eyes

i look at you with all the light and the darkness i possess

APUNTES PARA UNA CONFESIÓN
CON RUTABAGAS

The first of the undecoded messages read:
"Popeye sits in thunder, unthought of"
—John Ashbery

Castor Oil: Hey there! Are you a sailor?
Popeye: Ja think I'm a cowboy?
Castor Oil: O.K. You're hired.
—Elzie C. Segar

[1]
escribo mejor cuando no hay luz cuando es muy tarde
y no hace ruido aparecen las palabras libres limpias se
descuelgan de las ramas abren puertas caminan por el techo
anoche vi una se llama rutabagas no sé qué significa la leí
en el mercado la leí en un poema me gusta esa palabra
sabe a caminos extraviados a relojes perdidos en orión
nunca me he extraviado nunca he perdido relojes en orión
ya veo es así como mientes así como te dejas engañar

[2]
las espinacas no me gustan son tan verdes tan dulzonas
saben a comida de hospital a flores místicas y sucias
tienes fiebre estás delirando no no tengo fiebre no estoy
delirando la memoria es como el miedo levanta enormes
catedrales luego las destuye estoy cansado escucho voces
es la fiebre que lame mi cuerpo es olivia diciéndome al oído
soy tu fantasía tu inútil y hermosa debilidad

NOTES FOR A CONFESSION
WITH RUTABAGAS

The first of the undecoded messages read:
"Popeye sits in thunder, unthought of"
—John Ashbery

Castor Oil: Hey there! Are you a sailor?
Popeye: Ja think I'm a cowboy?
Castor Oil: O.K. You're hired.
—Elzie C. Segar

[1]
i write better when there isn't any light when it's very late
and there's no noise the words show up free and clean then
dangling from branches opening doors walking on the rooftop
last night i saw one called rutabagas i don't know what it means
i read it in the marketplace in a poem somewhere i like the word
it smacks of trails off the beaten path of clocks lost in orion
i've never wandered off the beaten path never lost clocks in orion
i see so that's the way it is you liar just keep fooling yourself

[2]
i don't like spinach it's so green so cloyingly sweet
it tastes like hospital food like dirty mystical flowers
you have a fever you're raving no i don't i'm not
raving memory is like fear it erects enormous cathedrals
only to knock them down i'm tired i hear voices
it's the fever licking my body olive whispering in my ear
i'm your fantasy your lovely ineffectual weakness

[3]
mejor no continuar el mensaje cifrado decía popeye
se sienta indiferente sobre el trueno escucha nadie
se sienta indiferente sobre el trueno nadie recuerda
ese episodio la moneda que hundió el barco los cuarenta
ladrones persiguiendo a olivia su propensión a la lujuria
no se perderá en el desierto no devorará tinieblas no
se hundirá en el mar

[4]
batman me mira escribir su fuerza viene de la noche
del descontento viene nunca dice nada sólo aprueba
o desaprueba es implacable cómo ruge su automóvil
cómo abolla cubos de basura espanta gatos callejeros
se detiene en esquinas solitarias bebe el agua de los
charcos se masturba en oscuros edificios pero nunca
dice nada como el ángel nunca dice nada

[5]
estoy un poco confundido dijo popeye batman alza un pie
hunde el otro en ciudad gótica arroja un chorro de luz negra
en esta habitación vacía no es verdad no está vacía hay
libros papeles diccionarios un póster de national geographic
una taza de café humea en lo más alto me mira escribir
una sextina quieres escucharla ahora no dijo popeye
estoy un poco confundido ¿por qué hablas de batman?

[6]
es un amuleto me lo regaló por mi cumpleaños
cuando me vaya se quedará contigo dijo y se fue
dejándome esta niebla esta mirada de murciélago

[3]

it's best not to continue the coded message read popeye
sits in thunder unthought of he's listening no one
sits in thunder unthought of no one remembers that
episode with the coin that sank the ship and the forty
thieves chasing after olive her propensity toward lust
will not be lost in the desert will not devour the darkness
will not sink to the bottom of the sea

[4]

batman watches me write his strength comes from the fall
of day from his own unhappiness never saying a word he just
shakes his head yes or no inexorable though his batmobile sure
does roar denting garbage cans and frightening alley cats
he stops on solitary street corners drinking water from the
puddles masturbating in unlighted buildings but never
saying a word like the angel he never says a word

[5]

i'm a little confused popeye said batman lifts one foot and
buries the other into gotham city shooting a stream of black light
into this empty room that's not true it's not empty there are
books here paper dictionaries a national geographic poster
a cup of steaming coffee from high in the air he watches me
write a sestina would you like to hear it not now popeye said
i'm a little confused why are you talking about batman?

[6]

it's a good-luck charm she gave me for my birthday
you'll always have it when i go away she said and away
she went leaving me with this fog and bat-like image

[7]
hey me preguntó tú eres marino ¿acaso parezco un cowboy?
así empezó todo esa misma tarde salimos a la mar no había
tripulantes fregué con un trapo la cubierta levé anclas limpié
las escotillas era el año veintinueve tú no habías nacido olivia
era un estorbo le tuvimos que rogar que se quedara me pregunta
dibujar es distinto a escribir no no es distinto ella vive en otra
esfera habla en demótico las palabras arden en su lengua deja
migajas en la lluvia agujeros en los libros así es olivia de noche
viene se va cuando amanece ¿alguno de ustedes sabe dónde está?

[8]
búscala en el diccionario es comestible su nombre
rutabagas napus naprobrassica buena para la digestión
me gusta la palabra digestión dijo olivia mostrando
un seno diminuto dijo batman en un rapto de locura
la repite y vuelve a significar lo mismo otro mensaje
cifrado el cielo opalino la noche fría y sin estrellas
todo invita a la contemplación todo excepto olivia

[9]
el diccionario susurra su luz insiste está llena de huecos
me ofrece la palabra equinoccio la palabra alegoría no lo
escucho allá en el sur es primavera en el norte comienza
el otoño eso ya lo sé las hojas caen se vuelven amarillas
los pájaros devoran ratones y gusanos las madres abrigan
a sus hijos se desvisten sin que nadie las vea olivia se hace
de rogar estoy cansado le digo no me gusta el otoño no
quiero terminar mis espinacas no quiero escribir este poema

[7]
hey there he asked are you a sailor ja think i'm a cowboy?
that's how it all began we set sail that very afternoon there was
no crew so i swabbed the deck with a rag weighed anchor cleaned
the hatches that was nineteen twenty-nine you weren't born yet olive
i was a hindrance we had to beg him to let me stay she asks me
drawing is different from writing right no it's not she lives in another
world speaks a demotic language the words burn on her tongue she
        leaves
behind crumbs in the rain holes in books that's olive she comes by
at night and leaves at dawn do any of you know where she is?

[8]
look it up in the dictionary you can eat it its name is
rutabagas napus naprobrassica good for the digestion
i like the word digestion olive said showing off
a diminutive breast batman she said in a state of rapture
she repeats this but it means the same another coded
message the opalescent sky the cold starless night
everything invites contemplation everything except olive

[9]
the dictionary whispers its light it's insistent and filled with gaps
offering me the word equinox the word allegory though i don't listen
in the southern hemisphere it's springtime while in northern climes
autumn is just beginning i know the leaves fall and turn yellow
while the birds devour mice and worms mothers bundle up
their children and undress themselves unseen then olive starts
pleading with me i'm tired i tell her i don't like autumn don't
want to finish my spinach don't want to write this poem

[10]
si arrojas tu amuleto a la basura si abres las ventanas
si pudieras despertarte de una vez si eligieras
con cuidado tus palabras si pudieras contestarme

cuando te hablo tal vez vuelva contigo no lo olvides
soy tu fantasía tu inútil y hermosa debilidad

[10]

if you throw away your good-luck charm and open the windows
if you could just wake up for once and choose your words
with care if you would only answer me

when i speak to you then maybe i'll come back but don't forget
i'm your fantasy your lovely ineffectual weakness

EL LIBRO DE LA VIDA O MIS CONVERSACIONES CON TERESA DE JESÚS

Para Pepa Merlo y Álvaro Salvador

No sé si hago bien de escrivir tantas menudencias

[1]
escribo para salvar mi vida para que me perdones escribo
siempre a vuelapluma siempre mirando al cielo siempre
mirando al techo de cualquier lugar puede venir su boca
es espantable su llama clara y sin sombra así es como
aparece así como seduce yo no me dejo engañar le arrojo
agua bendita me santiguo pero hablemos de ti sabes de
memoria esa música leíste ya todos los libros iba a seguir
la carne es triste pero sé de dónde vienes a mí no podrás
engañarme aunque quieras a mí no podrás engañarme

[2]
el sonido es anterior a la palabra dibuja entonces
la palabra el sonido llega con la música no entiendo
toma un poco de algodón y haz una oveja pinta
los ojos me decía pinta el miedo la cola las orejas
estaba tan nervioso no sabía qué hacer de pronto
balaba de pronto brincaba recuerdo esa música
el horror de la maestra el castigo de mis padres el niño
que fui ha muerto decía aprende esto es un poema

THE BOOK OF MY LIFE OR MY CONVERSATIONS WITH SAINT TERESA OF ÁVILA

For Pepa Merlo and Álvaro Salvador

I don't know whether I am doing right to enter into such trivial details

[1]
i write so as to save my life so that you'll forgive me i write
always my quill pen flying always looking heavenward always
at the ceiling his mouth can come out of nowhere it's fearsome
that bright shadowless flame of his that's how he appears how
he seduces i don't allow myself to be deceived throw holy water
at him make the sign of the cross but let's talk about you do you
    know
that music by heart have you read every book yet i was about to
    continue
the flesh is sad but i know whence you come for me you won't be able
to deceive me try as you like you won't be able to deceive me

[2]
the sound precedes the word so go ahead then draw
the word the sound comes with the music i don't understand
take some cotton and make a sheep paint
its eyes she said paint its fear its tail its ears
i was so nervous i didn't know what to do suddenly
it bleated suddenly it skipped about i remember that music
the teacher's horror the punishment from my parents the boy
i was has died she said learn this is a poem

[3]

ayer mientras oraba el demonio se sentó sobre mi libro
le dije que se fuera es tan fuerte su olor quiero estar sola
me dijo también tengo visiones veo hormigas despeñándose
en el fuego un león agonizando entre las llamas le dije
no lo sabes esa imagen es la tuya mi camino no conduce
a la belleza yo busco la verdad no me dijo tú morirás
por la belleza yo me pudriré para siempre en la verdad

[4]

con la lentitud del lagarto y la sabiduría del mono
con la sagacidad del gato y la discreción del cuervo
así aparece me pisa los talones araña mi espalda sopla
mis orejas muerdo hasta sangrar mis labios me llama
por mi nombre no volteo es abominable es tan hermosa
la cara de la muerte

[5]

acércate y cuéntame de nuevo la historia con trozos
de algodón debía crear una oveja era un niño no sabía
leer no sabía escribir de pronto saltó de mis papeles
comía de mi mano su música oscurecía las palabras
no había palabras brincaba en los jardines olisqueaba
flores tenía tanto miedo el león se le ocurrió a gregorio
su león era una hormiga murió por no tener su presa

[6]

ayer mientras oraba vi una gran contienda los demonios
luchaban con los ángeles no podía entender esa visión
las aves se arrastraban como sierpes decían en su lengua
no hay lugar para los ángeles no existen los demonios
las sierpes se enroscaban en mi cuello decían en su lengua

[3]

yesterday as i was praying the devil sat on my book
get thee hence i said his smell is so strong i want to be alone
he told me i have visions too i see ants tumbling headlong
into fire a lion in the throes amid the flames i told him
you don't know it but that image is yours my road does not lead
to beauty i seek the truth he did not say to me you will die
for beauty's sake i will rot forever in the truth

[4]

with the creep of a lizard and the cunning of a monkey
with a cat's shrewdness and a crow's discretion that's how
he appears trampling me his claws scratching my shoulders
he blows into my ears i bite my lips until they bleed he calls me
by my name i don't turn around the face of death is abominable
yet ever so lovely

[5]

come nearer and tell me again that story with the cotton
balls i was to fashion a sheep i was only a boy couldn't
read or write suddenly it jumped off the sheets of paper
ate from my hand its music drowning out the words
there were no words it skipped about in the gardens sniffed
flowers felt such great fear the lion it occurred to gregory
his lion was an ant that perished for lack of prey

[6]

yesterday as i was praying i saw a fierce battle the demons
were fighting the angels i didn't understand the vision birds
dragged their bodies along like serpents saying in their language
that there is no place for angels that demons don't exist
the serpents curled around my neck saying in their language

no irás a ningún cielo no habitarás ningún infierno yo
cerré su libro yo temblé de amor a dios

[7]
¿por qué hablas de los ángeles? nunca he visto uno jamás
me han visitado los demonios deberían dice no la escucho
escribe ligero escribe menudencias así es como las llama
yo me aferro a mi lenguaje es inútil no hay lenguaje
el león agoniza la oveja danza en una cartulina rosa

[8]
aunque quiera no puedo irme he esperado siglos para verte
mira mis pies enrojecidos mis manos hinchadas de tanto
rezar y rezar mira las nubes son ellas mi descuido de niña
convencí a mi hermano queríamos ser libres huir de casa
ver tierra de moros a mi hermano lo mataron en el sur
fue hace tanto tiempo no recuerdo su cara he olvidado
su nombre

[9]
difícil vivir con una santa escribe a vuelapluma ve demonios
conversa con los ángeles ayer soñé que estaba en galilea
vi a cristo jesús ávidas muchedumbres lo rodeaban apenas
lo podía ver yo estaba sola todo alrededor era desierto
luces huecas atravesando mi alma y un negrillo abominable
quemando mis pajitas no entiendo debes ser más clara
el cielo es gris cuando amanece azul cuando hace sol naranja
por las tardes no te dejes engañar el cielo es siempre azul
y él es legión así se llama de cualquier lugar puede venir
esta noche tengo miedo esta noche quédate conmigo

you will not go to any heaven not dwell in any hell i
closed his book trembling from the love of god

[7]
why are you talking about angels? i've never seen one ever demons
have visited me though they ought to have she says but i don't listen
she writes about minor things trivial details is what she calls them
i stand by my language it's pointless there is no language
the lion in the throes the sheep dancing on pink cardboard

[8]
i can't leave much as i'd like to i've waited ages to see you
look at my feet all red my hands swollen from all that
praying and praying look at the clouds my girlhood distraction
i convinced my brother we wanted to be free run away from home
see the land of the moors they killed my brother in the south
it was so long ago i can't remember his face have forgotten
his name

[9]
it's hard to live with a saint who writes her quill pen flying sees
    demons
converses with angels yesterday i dreamt i was in galilee
saw christ jesus enthusiastic crowds surrounded him i could
hardly see him there alone with desert all around me
hollow lights piercing my soul and an abominable black imp
burning my hay for kindling i don't understand you should be clearer
the sky is gray at dawn blue when there is sunshine orange
in the evenings don't be fooled the sky is always blue
and he is legion that's his name he can come out of nowhere
tonight i'm afraid stay with me tonight

[10]
con la lentitud del lagarto y la sabiduría del mono
con la sagacidad del gato y la discreción del cuervo
así aparece me pisa los talones acaricia mi espalda besa
mis orejas borra una por una las palabras de su libro
no sé si hago bien de escribir tantas menudencias

[10]
with the creep of a lizard and the cunning of a monkey
with a cat's shrewdness and a crow's discretion that's how
he appears trampling me his claws caressing my shoulders
he kisses my ears erases the words from his book one by one
i don't know whether i am doing right to enter into such trivial details

FÁBULA DE LA ALONDRA Y LA LUNA

Mit allen Augen sieht die Kreatur
das Offene
—*Rainer Maria Rilke*

do naszych domów wchodzi pełnia
—*Adam Zagajewski*

[1]
escribo en esta habitación donde no hay nadie donde nadie
perturba esta luz esta página tan sucia esta noche no estoy
solo mi madre elige un vestido mi padre lee el diario ayer
ha muerto santa brígida san owen visitó el purgatorio ¿qué
sabes tú del purgatorio? una multitud camina detrás de las
vidrieras recuerdo la lluvia la estatua escarchada por el frío
la luna llena sus cráteres azules el mar de la tranquilidad

[2]
ayer estuve en segovia callecitas empinadas cielo azul
turistas quejándose del frío nadie puede verlo al pie del
acueducto una loba amamantaba dos cachorros con qué
voracidad mordían sus pezones la leche blanca de la luna
nadie puede verlo la calle ardía el cielo ardía la alondra
volaba hacia el este con júbilo más bien con indiferencia

[3]
alguien no sé quien dibuja con torpeza mi destino torres
de piedra donde asoma la luna cuenta de nuevo la historia
un hombre espera en la estación lleva consigo un puñado
de nieve una hoguera una rosa cortada me dice te regalo

FABLE OF THE LARK AND THE MOON

Mit allen Augen sieht die Kreatur
das Offene
—Rainer Maria Rilke

do naszych domów wchodzi pełnia
—Adam Zagajewski

[1]
i write in this room where no one else bides where no one
disturbs this light this really dirty page tonight i'm not alone
mother picks out a dress while father reads the paper yesterday
st. bridget died and st. owen visited purgatory what do you
know about purgatory? a crowd walks by on the other side of the
shop windows i remember the rain the statue covered in frost
the full moon with her blue craters and sea of tranquility

[2]
yesterday i was in segovia with its steep narrow streets blue sky
and tourists complaining of the cold no one can see the sky at the foot
of the aqueduct where a she-wolf suckled two cubs biting
truly ravenously at her teats the white milky way of the moon
no one can see them there the street was ablaze the sky too as the lark
flew toward the east not so much in jubilation as indifference

[3]
someone i don't know who is clumsily plotting my destiny stone
towers where the moon's face pokes through tell the story again
a man waiting at a station carries with him a fistful of
snow a bonfire a freshly cut rose tells me this line of verse

este verso cuenta sus sílabas respira el aire tauro el aire
pez mira la tierra acumulada el surco vacío y tenebroso
la alondra ciega negada por el sol negada por la luna

[4]
nadie responde tus palabras giran como plumas como astros
perdidos en un desfiladero la rosa se marchita la hoguera
se apaga columnas de nieve se desploman me pregunta
qué hacer con el silencio qué hacer con los significados

[5]
es domingo mi madre se prueba zapatos mi padre espera
san owen se masturba al pie del purgatorio yo me aburro
leo una historieta la estatua del rey derribada por los monjes
la cruz de hierro mojada por la lluvia diez caballeros juran
venganza en una lengua incomprensible hace frío afuera hace
frío adentro la alondra se espanta de sí misma raya en zigzag
la porcelana de rilke no te engañes la alondra se eleva hacia
el sol ignora lo abierto desgarra un fondo de cortinas rojas

[6]
la luna cuelga silenciosa de un alambre así te acompaño
dice velaré tu sueño tu leve resplandor yo la acaricio
con ternura le digo que se vaya que la esperan allá lejos
donde duerme mi mujer y mi madre y todos mis hermanos

[7]
de qué hablas cuando no hablas me trago la lengua me cubro
los oídos es muy fácil miro la tierra que abandona el arado el
vuelo jubiloso de la alondra luego los olvido con qué destreza
los olvido cuestión de no ver cuestión de no escuchar cómo

is my gift to you count its syllables breathe in the taurus air the pisces
sky look at the mound of soil the gloamy empty furrow
the blind lark turned away by the sun rejected by the moon

[4]
no one replies your words swirl round like feathers like stars
lost in a gorge the rose wilts on the vine the bonfire dies out
columns of snow come falling down he asks me what
is there to do with silence what is there to do with meaning

[5]
it's sunday and mother is trying on shoes while father waits
st. owen masturbates at the gates of purgatory feeling bored
i read a comic strip with the king's statue toppled by monks
and the iron cross soaked by rain ten knights swear
vengeance in an unintelligible tongue it's cold outside cold
inside too the lark frightening itself makes a zigzag pattern
on rilke's porcelain but don't be fooled the lark ascends toward
the sun unfamiliar with open spaces tearing a backdrop of red
    curtains

[6]
the moon hangs silently from a wire that's how i'll be with you
she says keeping watch over your sleep your quiet radiance i caress her
lovingly tell her to go as people are waiting for her way over there
where my wife my mother and all my brothers and sisters lie asleep

[7]
what are you talking about when you're not talking i bite my tongue
cover my ears it's very easy i look at the soil the plow shunts aside and
the jubilant flight of the lark then i forget them using all my skill
i forget them it's simply a matter of not seeing of not hearing how

explicarlo en una callecita de segovia una loba amamanta dos
criaturas la primera dice mi nombre es ignorancia la segunda
mi nombre es el olvido

[8]
cuéntame de nuevo la historia un hombre estudia el horario
de los trenes lame con placer su propia sombra todo aquí
es distancia dice todo allí respiración las cosas del mundo
nos desbordan con qué terquedad volvemos a ordenarlas
ellas sabrán desordenarse le pregunto qué lleva a sus espaldas
el ocaso me responde soy yo quien debe despedirse quien
dice adiós adiós el hombre se hunde en la elegía dibuja con
el dedo un ocho en el serrín respira el aire tauro el aire pez

[9]
leo en una estampita de san owen si callo destrozará mi
lengua si cuento la historia devorará mis ojos una mano
ha escrito en el reverso yo quiero destrozar tu lengua yo
quiero devorar tus ojos

[10]
escribo en esta habitación donde no hay nadie donde nadie
perturba esta luz este remedo de luna con sus cráteres azules
su mar de la tranquilidad a esta hora américa duerme europa
camina indiferente detrás de las vidrieras alguien no sé quien
escucha lo que escribo me dice cada noche una alondra cruza
jubilosa por el cielo cada noche la luna entra silenciosamente
en nuestra casa

can i explain on a narrow street in segovia a she-wolf suckles two
babies the first says my name is ignorance the second
mine is oblivion

[8]
tell me the story again a man poring over a train schedule
licks his own shadow in pleasure everything here is far away
he says everything there a breath of fresh air the world's affairs are
bigger than we are through sheer stubbornness we put them in
     order again
they'll know how to break apart i ask him what he's carrying on his
     back
the sunset he replies i'm the one who needs to take his leave who
says farewell farewell sinking into elegy the man draws an eight in
the sawdust with his finger breathing in the taurus air the pisces sky

[9]
on a prayer card of st. owen i read if i keep quiet he'll crush
my tongue if i tell the story he'll devour my eyes someone has
scrawled on the back of the card i want to crush your tongue i
want to devour your eyes

[10]
i write in this room where no one else bides where no one
disturbs this light this imitation moon with her blue craters
and sea of tranquility america is asleep at this hour europe walks
indifferently by on the other side of the shop windows someone i
     don't
know who listens to what i write telling me each night a lark flies
jubilant across the sky each night the moon silently enters
our house

FLORES Y MOSCAS PARA BERTHE MORISOT

Para Catalina González y Juan Felipe Robledo

Édouard Manet, Berthe Morisot, 1872.
Óleo sobre lienzo, París, Musée d'Orsay.

[1]
una maleza de lino un cerco de agua un ave zambulléndose
en las olas quebrando el horizonte y lo demás color aquella
tarde una hortensia brotó entre marthe y jeanne-marie no
tuve más remedio que pintarla invocar sus hojas elípticas
y agudas su delicada corola que sostiene el mundo ahora
debo cerrar los ojos contar hasta diez y esperar el fogonazo
azul el fogonazo rojo ¿alguna vez has visto el fogonazo rojo?
una vez al borde mismo del sueño de los ojos negros o azules
de berthe morisot

[2]
entre el ojo y la imagen la pintura se deslíe rompe con
los dientes el cepo de su sombra cobra vida en el museo
pero aquí no hay ninguna sombra no hay ningún museo
sólo una hortensia marchita un ojo cansado de mirar
y un espejo te voy a contar una historia había una vez
una muchacha conozco a esa muchacha retuvo la sombra
de su amante cubrió con barro su perfil lo endureció con
fuego y se sentó a esperar ¿dónde has leído esa historia?
en plinio tal vez en atenágoras el amor es un fracaso que
busca eternizarse un cesto de frutas a punto de podrirse

FLOWERS AND FLIES FOR BERTHE MORISOT

For Catalina González and Juan Felipe Robledo

Édouard Manet, Berthe Morisot, 1872.
Oil on canvas, Paris, Musée d'Orsay.

[1]
a tangle of linen a ring of water and a bird plunging
into the waves breaking the skyline with all the rest color that
afternoon a hydrangea bloomed between marthe and jeanne-marie i
had no choice but to paint it to summon forth its pointy elliptical
leaves its slender corolla bearing the weight of the world now
i must close my eyes count to ten and wait for the flash
of blue the flash of red have you ever seen a flash of red?
once on the edge of sleep dreaming of the ebon or deep blue eyes
of berthe morisot

[2]
somewhere between image and eye the painting dissolves bites off
the branch providing the shadows comes to life in the museum
but here there are no shadows here there is no museum
only a wilted hydrangea an eye grown weary from all its looking
and a mirror let me tell you a story once upon a time there was
a girl and i know that girl personally who held on to her lover's
shadow covered its contours with mud baked it hard over
fire then sat down to wait where did you read that story?
in pliny maybe in athenagoras love is a fiasco that
tries to last forever a basket of fruit on the verge of rotting

[3]

una multitud camina indiferente por la calle así comienza
el espectáculo gotas de lluvia golpeando la ventana un juego
perverso de visillos las ramas espesas de un álamo temblón
cualquier obstáculo es bueno si estorba la mirada si vuelve
nuestros ojos del revés los antiguos maestros lo sabían
la belleza es un capricho incesante de la forma y la forma
dibuja su danza en el vacío ahora junta la puerta aléjate
unos pasos y mira el abanico andaluz ¿puedes ver mis ojos?

[4]

una rosa azul flota a la distancia hiere sin dolor la levedad
del aire me pregunta por su mano derecha por su moño
peinado con esmero por su cuerpo que arde y me destruye
por las noches no sé qué contestarle sus ojos me observan
detrás del abanico enturbian para siempre la mirada

[5]

entre edma y yo florece una multitud de ángeles ella no
los ve de día desgarran en silencio el cortinaje resbalan
por los pliegues del vestido manchan las paredes de un
marrón oscuro borran con sus alas el pomo de la puerta
ahítos de color babean como perros de noche lamen la
blancura de sus piernas propician un escándalo de verdes
un estrépito de rojos

[6]

una mosca vuela distraída por el techo proyecta su sombra
en la blanca superficie del retrato desaparece al segundo y
al segundo vuelve a significar otra cosa tal vez no significa
nada es hermosa como aquello que nos hiere como aquello
que no significa nada

[3]
a crowd walks aimlessly through the streets that's how
the show begins with raindrops striking the windowpane
a perverse play of lace curtains the thick boughs of an aspen
any obstacle is fine if it obstructs the view if it turns
our eyes inward the old masters knew this beauty
is a ceaseless whim of form and form limns its dance
in the empty expanse now pull the door shut take a few
steps back and look at the andalusian fan can you see my eyes?

[4]
a blue rose floats off in the distance painlessly wounding
the lightness of the air she asks me about her right hand her
carefully coiffed topknot her body that burns and destroys me
in the night i don't know what to tell her behind the fan
her observing eyes cloud my gaze forever

[5]
a multitude of angels flower between edma and me she can't
see them during the day they silently tear the curtains slide
down the folds in our dresses leave dark brown stains on
the walls obscure the doorknob with their wings
in a surfeit of color drool like dogs in the night lick the
whiteness of their legs giving rise to a scandal of greens
a riot of reds

[6]
up by the ceiling a fly buzzes idly casts its shadow over
the portrait's white surface disappears for a second before
returning the next to mean something else perhaps it doesn't
mean a thing it's lovely like that which wounds us like that
which doesn't mean a thing

[7]

dice eugenio en los ojos de berthe morisot una flecha
ignora para siempre el esplendor de su arco dice eduardo

en los ojos de berthe morisot un cuchillo corta el vuelo
de una mosca el crecimiento implacable de una flor

[8]

desplegar un paisaje inmune a la ceguera al humo que aturde
la pantalla y acaricia sin miedo los colores la tersura del rojo
la aspereza del verde la obscenidad del amarillo quien toque
mi cuerpo verá crecer una flor he pintado infinidad de flores
tras la niebla que brilla tras las moscas del deseo tras los ojos
que duelen al mirarme

[9]

aquella noche se rebelaron las palabras me dijeron no
somos responsables nos inquietan tus trampas mejor
el desconcierto la afonía del sentido estaba cansado
no sabía qué decirles un gorjeo inútil tal vez un estertor
de pájaros una mosca volaba por el techo los ángeles
lucían aburridos les pregunté por qué no se quedaban
es tarde me dijeron a ti te aguarda el final de este poema
los ojos negros o azules de berthe morisot

[10]

entre marthe y jeanne-marie crece una hortensia entre
eduardo y eugenio dos gladiolos entre edma y yo una rosa
azul que no se pinta que no florece

[7]
eugène says in berthe morisot's eyes an arrow
remains forever unaware of its arc édouard says

in berthe morisot's eyes a knife slices through a fly's
trajectory cuts down a flower's inexorable growth

[8]
to lay out a landscape immune to blindness to the smoke that
    overwhelms
the screen and to caress its colors without fear the smoothness of
    the red
the roughness of the green the obscenity of the yellow whoever
    touches
my body will see a flower grow i've painted countless flowers
at the back of the glistening fog of the flies of desire of the eyes
pained to look at me

[9]
that night the words rose up in rebellion told me we're not
responsible your tricks trouble us better for disorder
to reign for meaning to lose its voice i was tired i didn't know
how to answer them with some futile warbling perhaps or
the death rattle of birds a fly buzzed up by the ceiling the angels
looked bored i asked them why they were leaving
it's late they said and the end of this poem awaits you
the ebon or deep blue eyes of berthe morisot

[10]
a hydrangea grows between marthe and jeanne-marie two
gladioli between édouard and eugène but between edma and me
a blue rose that will never be painted that never will flower

ATANASIO Y EL ARCA O
LA CONVERSIÓN DE SAN EUSTAQUIO

. . . cuando Dios llevó todos los animales
ante Adán para que les pusiera nom-
bre, no se estaba refiriendo a todos los
animales que con el correr de los tiempos
iban a llenar el mundo, sino a aquellos
que Dios había creado, no a los que pos-
teriormente habían de surgir, a los que
no había razón para poner nombre.
—Athanasius Kircher

[1]

en esta ruinas cristo jesús se apareció a san eustaquio
plácido le dijo ¿podrías decir un trabalenguas? el obispo
de constantinopla me ordenó construir este santuario
nada queda en pie sólo un árbol seco algunas piedras y
una inscripción noviembre de mil seiscientos ochenta
ahora lo sabes qué más quieres de mí quiero un poema
que hable del diluvio las aguas que arrasaron la sepultura
de dante apenas lo recuerdo en estas ruinas he olvidado
mis despojos en estas ruinas he abandonado mi nombre

[2]

esta noche iremos al lugar donde callaron tus perros
dirás una plegaria el trabalenguas que habla de los tigres
me gustan los tigres los he visto en el palacio de mogor
parecen gatos ligeros y veloces cuando aprieta el hambre
indolentes y vagos si se encuentran satisfechos en china
los consideran peligrosos sus bocas despiden un veneno
irrespirable sus pieles arruinan toda perfección

ATHANASIUS AND THE ARK OR
THE CONVERSION OF SAINT EUSTACE

. . . when God brought all the animals
before Adam so he might give them
names, this did not entail all the
animals which over the course of time
came to populate the earth, but only those
God had created up to then, not the ones
that were to appear in later ages, to which
there was no need to give names.
—Athanasius Kircher

[1]
amid these ruins christ jesus appeared to saint eustace
placidus he said can you tell me a tongue twister? the bishop
of constantinople ordered me to erect this sanctuary
nothing remains standing only a dry tree some rocks and
an inscription november anno domini sixteen hundred eighty
now you know what more do you want from me i want a poem
that tells of the flood the waters that washed dante's tomb
away i can hardly remember amid these ruins i have forgotten
my plunder amid these ruins i have abandoned my name

[2]
tonight we'll go to the spot where your dogs fell silent
and you'll say a prayer that tongue twister about the tigers
i like tigers i saw them once in the mughul palace
lithe and lissome cats when hunger gnaws at them
more like indolent and lazy beasts when well-fed in china
they're considered dangerous with mouths that spew
a venom deadly to breathe their pelts annulling all perfection

[3]

ya veo te gusta hablar de animales hablemos entonces del
perro de bubastis del chivo mendesio hablemos si quieres
del tragelafo hijo del macho cabrío con la cierva tiene los
cuernos azules de su madre el olor hediondo de su padre
aristóteles habló del cruce del potro salvaje y la gacela
pero jamás lo vio como tampoco vio al bastardo del mono
con la zorra que tiene pies humanos y orejas de murciélago
ni al cruce de hiena con león que llaman leocrota ninguno
conserva su nombre ninguno tuvo lugar en el arca

[4]

tu dios era un ciervo lo perseguía con saña cazarlo era
el sentido de mi vida la razón de mi nombre he olvidado
mi nombre hay cosas que no puedo comprender en malta
vi un animal monstruoso mezcla de cuadrúpedo con ave
tenía cuello de jirafa joroba de camello tenía alas inútiles
de pájaro dicen que es glotona que habita los desiertos
que oculta sus huevos en la arena y después los abandona
hay cosas que no puedo comprender en job está escrito
ese monstruo tuvo lugar en el arca

[5]

hace tiempo quería preguntarte por tu nombre no tengo
ningún nombre el que tenía lo olvidé hace siglos si quieres
saber pregúntale a la luna cada noche viene a visitarme deja
en mi boca su escarcha su oscuro resplandor entonces te llamas
isidoro me dijo don de isis hijo de nadie regalo de la divinidad

[6]

un ejército de ángeles ensaya la expulsión del paraíso
uno porta en sus manos el omega otro una a mayúscula

[3]
i see you like to talk about animals let's talk about the
dog from bubastis the mendesian goat let's talk if you like
about the tragelaph the offspring of a billy goat and doe
it has its dam's blue horns and sire's foul stench
aristotle spoke about the cross between a wild colt and gazelle
but never saw one himself like he never saw the mixed-breed
monkey and fox with its human feet and bat's ears or
the cross between a hyena and lion they call the leocrota not
a one has kept its name not a one found a place on the ark

[4]
your god was a stag i pursued with a vengeance hunting it down and
persecuting it was the meaning of my life the reason for my name i've
forgotten my name there are things i just can't understand in malta
i saw a monstrous animal once a mix of quadruped and fowl
with a giraffe's neck a camel's hump and a bird's wings though
these were useless it's ravenous they say and lives in the desert
hiding its eggs in the sand then abandoning them there
are things i just can't understand in job it is written
that this monster found a place on the ark

[5]
i've been meaning to ask your name for some time now i don't have
a name the one i had i forgot centuries ago if you'd like to
know it ask the moon that comes to visit me each night leaving
behind its hoarfrost and dark resplendence in my mouth you must be
isidor he said a present from isis no one's child a gift from god on high

[6]
a host of angels rehearses the expulsion from paradise
one carries the omega in its hands another a capital a

la dorada serpiente que muerde su cola y en el centro
el rostro de dios padre su ojo infalible que todo lo vigila
y tú ¿qué ves? veo naves incendiadas a lo lejos un palacio
de cristal la columna de hielo que maravilló a brendano
inscripciones en una lengua extraña nidos de sirena veo
peces ahogados de color naranja

[7]
por entretenerme manoteo un moscardón bebo un vaso
de agua repito de memoria los nombres en árabe llaman
zephet a la resina la palabra hebrea para cedro es gopher
el betún era petróleo dioscórides lo explica en sodoma
florecen torres de petróleo también en babilonia en las
riberas oscuras del mar muerto los soldados bombardean
beirut esta noche el humo oscurece la vista destruye las
paredes del arca

[8]
mañana irás conmigo al observatorio veremos juntos
las estrellas ya sabes io ganímedes calisto luego bajaremos
de la mano una vez más me contarás la historia

[9]
cuando acorralé al ciervo dio un gran salto la tierra tembló
las aves huyeron espantadas los perros dejaron de ladrar así
apareció cristo jesús brillaba entre los cuernos apenas
podía ver tan fuerte era el resplandor me dijo plácido ¿por
qué me persigues? no supe responder mi nombre es eustaquio
patrón de cazadores protector de tempestades y tormentas

the gilded serpent biting its tail and in the center the face
of god the father with his infallible eye watching all and you
what do you see? i see ships on fire and in the distance a
crystal palace the pillar of ice that instilled such wonder
in brendan inscriptions written in a strange tongue sirens' nests
i see drowned orange-colored fish

[7]
i swat at a fly to wile away the time drink a glass of
water repeat from memory the name of things in arabic they
call resin zephet the hebrew word for cedar is gopher
bitumen was petroleum dioscorides explains it in sodom
petroleum towers flourish too in babylon on the
dark shores of the dead sea the foreign soldiers shell
beirut tonight the smoke dims the view destroys the
walls of the ark

[8]
tomorrow you'll go with me to the observatory and we'll gaze at
the stars together you know io ganymede callisto then descend
hand in hand and you'll tell me the story again

[9]
when i cornered the stag it leapt high in the air the earth shook
the birds flew away in fright and the dogs stopped barking that's
when christ jesus appeared shining so radiantly between its horns
i could hardly see so great was his resplendence placidus he asked
why do you persecute me? i didn't know what to tell him my name is
eustace the patron saint of hunters protector from tempests and
    storms

[10]

los que nunca ingresaron al arca los que restregaron sus
lomos en la puerta los que perdieron sus nombres cuando
la lluvia arreciaba los que vieron de cerca el rostro oculto
de la desesperación todavía existen pueblan los bestiarios
recorren oscuros laberintos habitan el miedo y la fantasía
de los hombres atanasio los registre san eustaquio los
proteja dios los tenga en su gloria

[10]

the ones that never entered the ark those that rubbed their
backs on its door the ones that lost their names forever once
the rain beat down those that viewed up close the hidden
face of desperation still exist populating the bestiaries
ranging through dark labyrinths inhabiting the fears and fantasies
of humankind may athanasius record them all saint eustace
keep them and god receive them in his glory

ORDENANDO LA BIBLIOTECA ANTES DE DORMIR

În piept
mi s-a trezit un glas străin
şi-un cântec cântă-n mine-un dor, ce nu-i al meu
—*Lucian Blaga*

[1]
tanto silencio me rodea esta noche escucho los rayos
de la luna chocar en mi ventana el ris ras del corazón
en la oreja de nada sirve mirar en blanco interrogar el
alma la voz de los antepasados muertos ellos vuelven
para vivir todavía un poco más para estar un momento
con nosotros su silencio me rodea esta noche tenemos
la música me dicen ¿tienes tú las palabras?

[2]
aquí no hay islas prodigiosas no hay cera que cubra
los oídos ningún mástil donde encadenar el cuerpo
sólo un mar sin costas un café tibio el gesto burlón
de las sirenas no entiendo por qué hablas de sirenas
lo que buscas está en cualquier supermercado en los
desechos industriales en los perros que ladran a la luna

[3]
¿alguna vez has escuchado el ladrido de los perros a
la luna? en un poema de silva en un poema de leopardi
queda la noche viuda canta con triste melodía miento

PUTTING MY LIBRARY IN ORDER
BEFORE BEDTIME

În piept
mi s-a trezit un glas străin
şi-un cântec cântă-n mine-un dor, ce nu-i al meu
—Lucian Blaga

[1]

such silence all about me tonight i listen to the rays
of the moon striking my window my heart's pitter-patter
in my ear it's pointless to stare into space questioning the
soul the voice of dead ancestors they come back
to live on a little still to stay a moment
with us their silence surrounds me tonight we have
the music they say do you have the words?

[2]

there are no wondrous isles here no wax for stopping up
ears no mast to which one can shackle a body only a sea
without coasts a lukewarm cup of coffee the mocking face
of sirens i don't understand why you are talking about sirens
what you're looking for can be found in any supermarket in
industrial waste in the dogs that bark at the moon

[3]

have you ever listened to dogs barking at
the moon? in a poem by silva in a poem by leopardi
the night is left a widow singing a sad melody i'm lying

en jauja los escuché ladrar toda la noche parecían
asustados después hubo temblor a la mañana siguiente
apareció un arco iris

[4]
la sordera educa el ojo enseña a calcular sin pesos ni
medidas desordena ritmos hace girar constelaciones
ya sabes geometría es belleza pero belleza es débil
llora al final de cada laberinto en cada playa donde
la abandona el héroe la han visto merodear tu casa
mendigar una moneda a veces llama por tu nombre
eduardo eduardo pero tú jamás escuchas

[5]
si quiero escuchar cierro los ojos es muy fácil lo aprendí
de niño veo manchas de lenguaje naves aqueas cruzando
el dormitorio el cráneo de helena que hermes le mostró
a menipo el rinoceronte que naufragó en liguria qué fue
de aquel rinoceronte no sé pregúntale a longhi a durero
pregúntale en venecia las máscaras se pudren se pudren
obscenamente danzan en una pista de baile

[6]
ayer ordenando la biblioteca apareció un verso no sé
por qué lo recordaba debo haberlo leído de joven tal
vez yo mismo lo escribí para olvidarlo después su música
sacude con rabia mis oídos es la peor manera de dormir
la más recomendable cómo aceptar un verso que golpea
la memoria hasta hacerla doler no te preocupes dice
si no recordaras cualquier otro me hubiera escrito

i heard them bark all night in jauja they seemed
frightened afterwards there was a tremor and the following
morning a rainbow appeared

[4]

deafness educates the eye teaches one to estimate without weights
or measures breaks up rhythms makes constellations spin round
you know that geometry is beauty but beauty is weak
it cries at the impasse in every labyrinth on every beach where
the hero abandons it they've seen it prowling around your house
begging for change sometimes calling you by name
eduardo eduardo but you never listen

[5]

when i want to listen i close my eyes it's very easy i learned to do
so as a child i see splashes of language achaean ships crossing
the bedroom helen of troy's skull which hermes showed
to menippus the rhinoceros shipwrecked in liguria what ever
became of that rhinoceros i don't know ask longhi or dürer
ask about it in venice the masks rot and rot away
moving obscenely over a dance floor

[6]

putting my library in order yesterday a verse came to me i don't
know why i remembered it i must have read it when i was young
maybe i wrote it myself only to forget it later its music
furiously drubs my ears which is the worst way to sleep
but the most advisable for welcoming a line of poetry that strikes
one's memory until it hurts don't worry it tells me if you
hadn't remembered anyone else could have written me

[7]
la noche se alarga como las páginas de un libro de nada
sirve contar una por una las ovejas de nada sirve mirar
por la ventana los negocios del mundo los perros ladran
a la luna las ovejas se arraciman frotan con descaro sus
pellejos reclaman cualquier número no puedo dormir
esta noche helena no ha venido el rinoceronte mastica
heno indiferente al público indiferente a los perros que
ladran y a la luna

[8]
mirar en blanco no es ninguna solución la espuma tiene
un límite tras la piel de la infanta se ve correr el vino la
ballena mancha con su sangre la pureza del hielo mi cabeza
arroja sombra en el papel oscurece cualquier verso hablas
de un lugar común el abismo donde mueren las ovejas
el humo sobre el tren que parte la turbia manquedad de
venus tienes la música ¿puedes esperar por las palabras?

[9]
esa música no es mía viene de muy lejos de épocas
remotas del primer rinoceronte que soñó venecia del
libro que alguna vez prestaste anoche tuve un sueño
ordenando mis papeles encontré un poema hablaba
del silencio lo leí en rumano yo nunca hablé rumano
no importa el silencio es igual en cualquier lengua
al despertar recordaba apenas unos versos y una sola
pregunta ¿en qué pecho cantarás cuando me vaya?

[10]
no pierdas el tiempo me dijo ésa es una pregunta inútil
y además no tiene ninguna respuesta

[7]

the night stretches on like the pages of a book it's no
use counting sheep one by one no use looking out
the window at the business of the world the dogs bark at
the moon the sheep cluster together shamelessly rubbing their
hides against one another don't care in what order they're counted
i can't sleep tonight helen has not come the rhinoceros chews
hay indifferent to the public indifferent to the dogs that
bark and to the moon

[8]

staring into space is no solution the foam has its limits
you can see wine flowing under the infanta's skin the
whale stains the ice's purity with its blood my head
casts a shadow on the paper darkens any verse you speak
of a common place the abyss where sheep die
the smoke above the departing train venus's turbid
defect you have the music can you wait for the words?

[9]

that music isn't mine it comes from far away from remote
eras from the first rhinoceros that dreamt of venice from the
book you once lent someone last night i had a dream
putting my papers in order i came across a poem that spoke
of silence i read it in romanian i've never spoken romanian
no matter silence is the same in any language
upon awakening i remembered a few lines and just one
question in whose breast will you sing when i'm gone?

[10]

don't waste your time it told me that's a pointless question
and besides it has no answer

TRECE INVIERNOS CON NIEVE

A blanker whiteness of benighted snow
With no expression, nothing to express
—Robert Frost

[1]
su mano de nieve saluda desde la ventana golpea de nuevo
la puerta es muy tarde le pregunto a qué has venido a vigilar
tu sueño me responde yo lo hago pasar le ofrezco chocolates
galletas de jengibre le ofrezco una taza de café sin ninguna
ceremonia se quita el sombrero los guantes la bufanda se
acomoda en el sillón ahora léeme un poema dice vengo
por la música desde hace trece años vengo por la música

[2]
el invierno son las agujas de una iglesia protestante un
cuervo sacudiendo la nieve en un poema de frost el lago
de hielo donde patinan las parejas no me dijo el invierno
son las olas del pacífico ballenas pudriéndose en las playas
pelícanos gaviotas y uno que otro pingüino en el perú
hay pingüinos ganas solemnes de no ir al colegio y un poco
de lluvia algo más un revuelo de zapatos escolares la tarea
pendiente en invierno los niños revientan ojos a los gatos
arrojan piedras a los perros

[3]
te cuesta trabajo no ser sentimental cedes fácilmente a
los recuerdos pero ésa no es la música debes concentrarte
un poco más mira el vacío de la página su densa y luminosa
blancura devorando sombras así cantaba mi abuela en su

THIRTEEN WINTERS WITH SNOW

A blanker whiteness of benighted snow
With no expression, nothing to express
—Robert Frost

[1]
his snowy hand waves through the window knocks on the door
again it's very late i ask him why have you come to watch over
your sleep he replies i let him in offer him chocolates
gingerbread cookies a cup of coffee and without more
ado he takes off his hat his gloves his scarf and settles
into the armchair now read me a poem he says i've come to
hear the music for thirteen years i've been coming for the music

[2]
winter is steeples on a protestant church a crow
shaking off that dust of snow in a poem by frost the
frozen lake where couples skate no he said winter
is the waves of the pacific whales rotting on beaches
pelicans seagulls a penguin here and there in peru
there are penguins solemn desires to cut class a little
rain and something else a flurry of school shoes homework
to be done in winter the kids poke out cats' eyes
throw rocks at dogs

[3]
you find it hard not to be sentimental succumb easily to
memories but that's not music you ought to concentrate
a little more look at the blankness of the page its dense glaring
whiteness devouring shadows this is how my grandmother sang

patio caía la nieve blanco sobre blanco como un paisaje
de john cage como la sucia ventana de malevich toma
una piedra rompe la sucia ventana de malevich escucha
su canción su insoportable silencio de cristales rotos

[4]
sin mayor entusiasmo le muestro fotos de familia tu madre
es demasiado joven no la imaginaba así tu padre luce tan
serio tan lejano se llama igual que tú no sabía que hubiera
muerto dos niñas lloran al lado del triciclo el muchacho de
barba debe ser tu hermano pero tal vez me equivoco y tu
mujer ¿dónde está tu mujer? está durmiendo dije y clavó
sus ojos en mi pene en el café que nos mantenía despiertos

[5]
todavía no empezamos silba una canción la primera
que venga a tu memoria pero no abras los ojos la música
vendrá sola como el agua como un aullido de claveles
como un estruendo de topacios

[6]
el tiempo se ha detenido no hay relojes no hay tampoco
calendarios qué más puedo decir no te preocupes soy yo
quien se traga los silencios quien hace las preguntas hace
años empezaste un poema no pudiste pasar del primer
verso en lima la niebla hace lo suyo destroza cualquier
página borra implacable las cenizas su blancura es ilusoria
la promesa del poema acabado la miseria del poema perfecto

[7]
aquella noche vimos el lago de hielo el paisaje holandés que
nos regala la muerte pasamos horas contemplando la iglesia

in her backyard the snow would be falling white on white like
some landscape by john cage like malevich's dirty window pick
up a rock and break malevich's dirty window listen to
its song the unbearable silence of its shattered glass

[4]
with no great enthusiasm i show him family photos your mother
is very young i had her pictured differently your father looks so
serious so distant the two of you have the same name i didn't know
he died two little girls are crying beside a tricycle the young man
with the beard must be your brother but maybe i'm wrong and your
wife where is your wife? she's sleeping i said as he fixed
his eyes on my penis on the coffee keeping us both awake

[5]
we still haven't begun whistle a tune any tune the first
that comes to mind but don't open your eyes the music
will come by itself like water like a howling of carnations
like a clamor of topaz

[6]
time is standing still there are no clocks around no calendars
either what more can i say don't worry i'm the one who
swallows silences the one who asks the questions years
ago you began a poem and couldn't get beyond the first
line in lima the mist does what it pleases destroys any page
it wishes implacably blots out the ashes its whiteness is illusory
so too the promise of the finished poem the perfect poem's failings

[7]
that night we saw the frozen lake the dutch landscape
gifting us death we spent hours looking at the protestant

protestante la torva cruz de hierro la corona de flores todo
es tan emotivo tan conmovedor no es más que un cuadro dije
una torpe alegoría religiosa no sabía que fueras religioso vivo
en otra esfera relegado por los dioses jamás nos molestamos
yo les ofrezco ignorancia les ofrezco indiferencia a cambio
ellos se ríen me arrojan piadosamente sus palabras

[8]
es inútil le dije no entiendo por eso he venido a visitarte
a decirte que nunca te llamarás horacio que nunca fuiste
herrero en la cubierta del arca nunca equilibrista en bayard
street esta noche he venido a escuchar el alfabeto del agua
su triste canción de ruiseñores estás diciendo que soy
un impostor no me dijo es inútil nunca entenderás nada

[9]
no estás atento debes concentrarte un poco más escucha
la maleza despuntando en la nieve el temblor silencioso
de las hojas la mancha que arruina el pentagrama vacío
te regalo esa imagen la mancha que arruina el pentagrama
vacío ¿quieres escuchar el poema que pediste?

[10]
no me dijo bostezando ya es hora de irse y tú debes dormir
tu mujer debe estar preocupada

church with its grim iron cross and garland of flowers everything
is so touching so moving it's only a painting i said
a trite religious allegory i didn't know you were religious i live
in another realm banished by the gods we never bother one another
i offer them ignorance show them indifference and in return
they laugh piously hurling their words at me

[8]
it's no use i told him i don't understand that's why i've come to visit
to tell you that your name will never be horacio that you were never
a blacksmith on the deck of the ark never a tightrope walker on bayard
street tonight i've come to listen to the water's alphabet
its sad nightingale song are you saying that i'm an impostor
no he said it's no use you'll never understand anything

[9]
you're not focusing try to concentrate a little more listen for
the weeds poking through the snow for the leaves' silent
fluttering for the stain that mars the empty pentagram
that image is my gift to you the stain that mars the empty
pentagram do you want to hear the poem you asked for?

[10]
no he said yawning it's time for me to leave and you should go to bed
your wife will be worried

EJERCICIOS PARA BORRAR LA LLUVIA

Until the Moss had reached our lips—
And covered up—our names—
—Emily Dickinson

[1]
el musgo enturbia mi boca enmudece mis labios cómo
empezar esta historia había una vez un libro recuerdo
apenas ese libro arrancaba sus hojas las veo perderse
rondar de noche tus almohadas hundirse en el enigma
de qué hablas me pregunta hablo de letras y de números
hablo de ejercicios que son tres de dónde vienen adónde
van por qué celebran la misma ceremonia el mismo olor
a frío la misma lluvia que creímos olvidada

[2]
es mediodía lo sé porque no hay sombra porque el sol
se ha detenido a contemplarnos su luz hiere mis ojos
enturbia las letras de su nombre no puedo recordar
su nombre se llamaba gauss se llamaba lobachevsky
de joven escribió un tratado de jardinería de viejo
le dijo no a euclides allí aprendimos todo es reducción
la torva mirada de la esfinge la sucia flor del algoritmo
la equis trazada en su piel con una caligrafía oscura

[3]
atraer el humo y no dejarse asfixiar he allí el primer
ejercicio ella leyó el poema con desgano noche tras
noche midiendo sus palabras sus mares sus silencios

EXERCISES FOR BLOCKING OUT THE RAIN

Until the Moss had reached our lips—
And covered up—our names—
—Emily Dickinson

[1]
the moss muddles my speech silences my lips how should
i begin this story once upon a time there was a book i barely
remember that book would rip out its pages i see them blowing away
now hanging about your pillows at night sinking into the enigma
what are you talking about she asks i'm talking about letters and
    numbers
about exercises three to be precise where they come from where
they are going why they celebrate the same ceremony the same smell
of cold the same rain we once believed to be long forgotten

[2]
it's noon i know because there's no shade because the sun
has stopped to observe us its light hurts my eyes
obscures the letters of his name i can't remember
his name was it gauss or maybe lobachevsky
as a young man he wrote a treatise on gardening when old
he rejected euclid there we learned about everything being
reduction about the sphinx's grim face the algorithm's filthy
flower the x drawn on skin in jet-black calligraphy

[3]
to attract smoke and not choke to death that's the first
exercise she read the poem reluctantly night after
night measuring its words its seas its silences i waited

esperé siglos su respuesta ella prefirió ser enigma
me amarás en sueños dijo olvidarás mi nombre borrarás
mis ojos y cuando todo sea ceniza volverá el poema
su luz ardiendo en mis noches como una bandera roja

[4]
no esperaba verla en el museo estaba sola cojeaba de un pie
hace tantos años le dije me dijo es verdad quería verte yo
también nos zambullimos en la alberca golpeamos el cristal
danzamos a orillas de un cielo improbable dos matrimonios
fracasados dos poemas balanceando sus pies en el vacío
cómo adormece el vacío cómo aviva el dolor la cicatriz
me pregunta qué dolor qué cicatriz

[5]
el cielo se apaga el sueño del lenguaje se desploma no hay
lugar para alguien como tú no entiendo qué significa alguien
como yo estamos en casa de mi abuela la perrita cocoa
mordisquea los zapatos señal de que hay visitas es mi tío
lo acompaña su novia desde hace tiempo la esperaba no
sé cómo explicarlo yo sabía su nombre yo veía en sus ojos
por qué no la saludas era un niño las palabras se hundieron
en mi lengua por primera vez me obligaron a cantar

[6]
la lluvia cae sobre tu libro cae sobre los techos de un país
lejano mezquitas minaretes medialunas y un turbante rojo
de mayor usaré turbante rojo me dejaré la barba tendré
conmigo un astrolabio ¿algo más? sí una sensación de frío
de okapis perdidos en el zoo de vergüenza por sumar
todavía con los dedos de rayar con la navaja la carpeta
de roble me acuerdo de la carpeta de roble me aburría

ages for her response but she preferred to be an enigma
you will love me in dreams she said forget my name blot out
my eyes and when everything is ash the poem will return
its light blazing like a red flag in my nights

[4]
i didn't expect to see her in the museum alone and limping
it's been a long time i said she said it's true i wanted to see
you too we dove into the pool took swipes at the mirror
danced on the banks of an unlikely heaven two failed marriages
two poems kicking their legs in the hollow of the void the
void can really make one sleepy the scar really revive the pain
what pain she asks what scar

[5]
the light in the sky dies down the dream of language crumbles there's
no place for someone like you i don't know what someone like me
means we're in my grandmother's house her puppy cocoa
is chewing on shoes a sign that guests are there it's my uncle
his girlfriend is with him i'd been waiting for her for some time i
don't know how to explain it i knew her name looked into her eyes
aren't you going to say hello i was only a boy the words sank
into my tongue and for the first time in my life forced me to sing

[6]
the rain falls on your book on the rooftops of a far-off
land with mosques minarets crescent moons and a red turban
when i grow up i'll wear a red turban let my beard grow long
carry around an astrolabe anything else? yes a feeling of cold
of okapis lost in the zoo of shame for still having to count
with my fingers for using a razor to cut the top of my oak
desk i remember the top of my oak desk bored with

en clase inventaba historias yo era el perro cristiano
el infiel que ignoraba los números

[7]
invocar el fuego y no dejarse quemar he allí el segundo
ejercicio primero vi sus pies estaba cansado tenía mucho
sueño mentira no estaba cansado no tenía mucho sueño
la fiesta había terminado me alegró tanto ver sus pies
así empezó todo la decisión de besarla de viajar juntos
por europa de tener hijos bailamos hasta el amanecer
le dije tú serás mi poema pero ella no me dijo nada

[8]
cerrar con fuerza los ojos y contar gaviotas he allí el tercer
ejercicio se trata de un asunto serio la lluvia adelgaza la pasión
decrece las manzanas se pudren en el bosque no entiendo
por qué hablas de manzanas por qué hablas del bosque soy
enigma me dice la esposa de tu tío ha muerto cómo sabes
le pregunto por la lluvia por la nieve por los pájaros

[9]
los niños apedreaban al cristiano perro le decían hueles mal
el cristiano no entendía se limitaba a sonreír con qué miedo
sonreía con qué miedo cerraba su libro el hombre del turbante
miraba la escena los niños volvían a apedrearlo nunca serás
como nosotros yo entregaba las pruebas en blanco lanzaba
lápices al techo hería cada noche su blancura

[10]
con cuánto sigilo me acercaba con cuánto temblor mordía
sus pechos me hundía en un viraje de plumas todo cedía

my classes i'd make up stories i was the christian cur
the infidel who did not know his numbers

[7]
to summon forth fire and not be burned that's the second
exercise first i saw her feet i was tired feeling really
sleepy that's a lie i wasn't tired didn't feel sleepy at all
the party had ended and seeing her feet made me so happy
that's how it all began the decision to kiss her to travel together
through europe to start a family we danced until dawn
i told her you will be my poem but she didn't say a word

[8]
to close one's eyes tight and count seagulls that's the third
exercise this is a serious matter the rain puts a damper on passion
reduces the crop of apples rotting in the woods i don't understand
why you're talking about apples why you're talking about woods i am
an enigma she tells me your uncle's wife has died how do you know
      that
i ask her about the rain about the snow about the birds

[9]
pelting the christian cur with rocks the boys yelled at him you smell
the christian didn't understand only smiled at them the fear he felt
smiling the fear he felt closing his book the man in the turban
watched this scene the boys started pelting him again you'll never be
like us i would hand in quizzes without a mark on them and toss
pencils at the ceiling tiles wounding their whiteness every night

[10]
how discreetly i approached her how i shook to nibble on
her breasts sinking into a swirl of feathers everything yielded

la suavidad de sus piernas el olor de su sexo el terciopelo
azul de su mirada esta noche huele a frío en berlín huele
a frío en lima en tokyo en nueva york cae la misma lluvia
el mismo enigma ha pasado tanto tiempo me pregunta
soy yo tu poema le digo sí tú eres mi poema

the softness of her legs the smell of her sex the blue
velvet of her gaze tonight it smells like cold in berlin smells
like cold in lima in tokyo in new york the same rain is falling
the same enigma so much time has passed us by she asks
am i your poem yes i say yes you are my poem

LO QUE DICE EL CANTO DE LOS PÁJAROS

Para Virginia Zavala y Víctor Vich

ma una storia non dura che nella cenere
e persistenza è solo l'estinzione
—Eugenio Montale

[1]
escoge el sueño lastimado donde arden los cuerpos o esa
voz que resiste al tiempo y a la trituración de los huesos
ella pidió la inmortalidad pero olvidó pedir la juventud
su carne se fue apagando hasta convertirse en polvo su
voz resurge desde la arena dispersa todo es signo me dice
el hierro candente de antiguas batallas las aves que anidan
alrededor de la carroña los perros que ladran de espaldas
a la luna

[2]
sobre el césped un payaso hace su pantomima inútil simula
arrojar a lo lejos una piedra y cae atravesado por un ciego
resplandor la palabra corrompe ese ciego resplandor el hálito
de vida que nos mantiene aferrados a un cuerpo a una isla
solitaria en medio del mar todo es signo repite la piedra
cae sobre mi espejo lo destroza en millones de fragmentos
regados en la playa como restos del naufragio

[3]
hace años soñé este poema llevo conmigo su dolor su
leyenda de barro deshaciéndose a mis pies construyendo
un jardín cerrado y absoluto era tan joven amaba la belleza

WHAT THE BIRDSONG SAYS

For Virginia Zavala and Víctor Vich

ma una storia non dura che nella cenere
e persistenza è solo l'estinzione
—*Eugenio Montale*

[1]
choose between the damaged dream where bodies burn and that
voice resistant to time to the grinding up of human bones
she asked for immortality but neglected to ask for eternal youth
so her flesh just wasted away into dust yet her voice rises
still from the scattered sand everything's a sign she says
the white-hot iron of ancient battles the birds nesting around
putrefying carrion the dogs that bark with their backs
to the moon

[2]
on the lawn a clown performs his pointless pantomime feigns
throwing a rock into the distance then falls pierced by a sightless
radiance the word corrupts this sightless radiance the breath
of life that keeps us lashed to a body to a solitary island
in the midst of the sea everything's a sign she repeats as the rock
falls to earth on my mirror shattering it into millions of pieces
strewn along the beach like the remains of a shipwreck

[3]
i dreamt this poem up years ago and carry with me its pain
its clay inscription falling apart at my feet fashioning a
garden closed and self-contained i was so young then i loved

su piadosa servidumbre leyéndome cartas en la nieve
diciéndome al oído que escriba pidiéndome que vuelva

[4]
su cuerpo era un río de noche inundaba el dormitorio
me ahogaba en las palabras decía qué arduo respirar en
cada verso transitar su sombra su bosque impenetrable
yo escuchaba sus ojos su quebrada voz cantando tras la
lluvia tras las piedras remotas y azules del acantilado

[5]
un leopardo bajaba cada noche hasta mi cama velaba
mi sueño lamía con cuidado mi rostro seré tu máscara
decía y me arrastraba por calles malolientes en busca
del amor yo borroneaba cientos de cuartillas rogaba
en tinieblas su ansiado resplandor pobre y suntuoso
lamento su fuerza hubiera derrotado ejércitos derribado
murallas conmovido el más seco y oscuro corazón

[6]
cuando al fin llegó trajo consigo todas las flores del mundo
con ellas debí construir un lecho un barco que supiera navegar
a la deriva pero olvidé las palabras ¿no tenía ya lo concedido?
la lluvia golpea no porque es la lluvia sino porque es monótona
mejor las olas que mueren al contacto con la orilla el violento
remolino que devora peces y estrellas en un horrendo afán

[7]
a la mañana siguiente hubo neblina era comienzos de verano
siempre hay neblina cuando comienza el verano se introduce
por los techos por debajo de las puertas estropea la ropa

beauty its pious servitude reading me letters in the snow
whispering in my ear that i should write asking me to come back

[4]
her body was a river that flooded my bedroom at night i was
choking on words how hard it must be she said to breathe in
every line to pass through each one's shading and impenetrable forest
i was listening to her eyes her cracking voice singing in back of
the rain in back of the steep cliff's rocks distant and blue

[5]
creeping down to my bed each night a leopard would watch
over my sleep and lick my face attentively i'll be your mask
it said dragging me through foul-smelling streets in search
of love i filled hundreds of sheets with scribblings pleaded
in the dark with love's poor longed-for radiance and sumptuous
lament its might could have vanquished armies brought
down walls softened the hardest and blackest of hearts

[6]
at last she arrived bringing with her all the flowers in the world
i was to fashion a bed out of them a boat capable of floating
adrift but i forgot the words hadn't i everything i'd wished for?
the rain drums down not because it's the rain but because it's
        monotonous
far better the waves that die out on contact with the shore the furious
eddy swallowing up fish and stars with the same horrendous zeal

[7]
the following morning the mist arrived it was the start of summer
and there is always mist when summer begins it floats in
through the rooftops beneath the doors ruining clothing

las sábanas las toallas luego se va y aparecen los pájaros qué
anémicos los pájaros nunca saben qué cantar no me dice no
sabes escucharlos es como hundirse en una ola siniestra como
dejarse arrastrar por caminos sin orillas sin los reconfortantes
bordes de la cama recuerda el frío los barrotes verticales de
hierro la muerte del lenguaje la muerte esplendorosa del amor

[8]
el amor es un puñal sombrío que afila cada noche su hoja
interminable sólo sabemos de su filo en el placer y el dolor
entre ellos vivimos a tientas esperando la revelación aquella
tarde vi el cuerpo de la diosa ardiendo de placer en el barro
se dejaba tocar por oscuros camelleros se retorcía de gozo
ante la vista de un avergonzado amante de noche no dormí
taché una por una las palabras las arrojé al canasto las olvidé
para siempre

[9]
un sombrío lucifer descendió sobre mi cama es hora me dijo
recoge tus maletas restregándome los ojos vi entre sueños
su fulgor sus alas mutiladas y negras de cansancio quién eres
pregunté no puedo recordar tu nombre yo soy quien esperas
dijo y se fue sacudiendo sus cenizas sus restos de naufragio

[10]
al alba el hielo se derrite los pájaros celebran el sol ellos
lo saben nada inmóvil hay sobre la tierra nada salvo tu ojo

towels sheets then it goes away again and the birds appear really
anemic birds that never know what to sing no she says you don't
know how to listen to them it's like diving into a treacherous wave like
letting yourself be dragged down shoreless paths without the
    comforting
edges of a bed remember the cold the iron bars sticking straight
up the death of language the splendored death of love

[8]
love's a grim dagger that sharpens its never-ending blade each
night we know of its edge only through the pleasure and pain we
live between groping our way along waiting for the revelation that
evening i saw the goddess her body burning with pleasure in the clay
letting herself be touched by dark-skinned camel-drivers squirming
    with joy
before the gaze of an embarrassed lover that night i couldn't sleep
    crossed
out words one by one and threw them into a wastepaper basket
    forgetting them
forever

[9]
a grim-looking lucifer plunked himself down on my bed it's time he
    said
pack your bags rubbing my eyes i saw from out the fog of dreams
his refulgence his mutilated wings black from weariness who are you
i asked i don't remember your name i'm the one you're waiting for he
said as he left shaking off his ashes and the remains of his shipwreck

[10]
at dawn the ice melts and the birds welcome the sun they
know nothing is motionless on earth nothing but your eye

su rumor hialino que ve pasar el agua los enigmas que a nadie
le interesa descifrar por qué escribes eso le pregunto hemos
leído tantas páginas compartido tanta nieve tanta soledad
mira las piedras duermen sobre cualquier imperfección
sobre cualquier teoría ellas lo saben nada hay sobre ti nada
sobre mí sólo un viejo poema sólo pájaros cantando

its transparent sound watching the water flow by the riddles no
one cares to solve why are you writing this i ask we've read
so many pages together shared so much snow so much solitude
look the rocks manage to sleep untroubled by imperfection
unperturbed by theory they know there's nothing above you
nothing above me just an old poem just birds singing

CARTAS QUE LLEGAN SIN HACER RUIDO

И море, и Гомер—все движется любовью
—*Osip Mandelstam*

Tes lettres de chaleur m'arrivent sans faire de bruit
—*Juan Larrea*

[1]
no la esfinge no quiere una respuesta quiere mi cara azul
mi vieja cara oscurecida por el sueño oscurecida por el
miedo a qué has venido me pregunta no sé qué contestarle
miro con vergüenza sus ojos el gesto agarrotado de su boca
sus interminables dientes de piedra ¿miraste lo que tenías
que mirar? ahora vete cuando vuelvas trae contigo una
hoguera un puñado de nieve una rosa cortada

[2]
aves negras vuelan por la playa peces muertos buscan
cadáveres de focas y delfines la historia de siempre tanta
rosa engatusada por el tiempo tanta lengua lamiendo
el roquerío borrando las formas del enigma no lo sabes
no hay ninguna forma no hay ningún enigma contempla
en silencio las aves admira su negror su oscura manera
de imponerse de día siguen la ruta migratoria de los astros
la turbia precisión de las mareas de noche se abandonan
al sueño me dejan dormir en un caballo blanco

[3]
las raíces deciden tomar aire se aburren de su encierro
de buscar cobijo bajo tierra de pronto asoman a la luz

LETTERS THAT ARRIVE WITHOUT FANFARE

И море, и Гомер—все движется любовью
—Osip Mandelstam

Tes lettres de chaleur m'arrivent sans faire de bruit
—Juan Larrea

[1]
no the sphinx doesn't want an answer she wants my blue face
my old face overshadowed by sleep overshadowed by fear
why have you come she asks i don't know how to answer
gazing ashamed into her eyes i see her mouth's strangled
expression her endless rows of stony teeth did you see what you
came to see? now go and when you come back bring with you a
burning stake a fistful of snow a freshly cut rose

[2]
black birds fly along the beach dead fish look for
the carcasses of seals and dolphins it's the same old story so
many roses wheedled by time so many tongues lapping
the rocks blurring the shapes of the enigma you don't know
there is no shape there is no enigma observe the birds
in silence admire their blackness their dark way of asserting
themselves by day they follow the stars' migratory pattern
the turbid precision of the tides by night they give themselves
over to dream and allow me to sleep on a white horse

[3]
the roots decide to come up for air bored by their confinement
by seeking shelter underground thrust all at once into the light

qué impudicia vegetal qué escándalo celeste las flores
celebran el prodigio las hojas caen al suelo se oscurecen
renuncian al favor supremo de los dioses ¿qué dicen
ahora las dalias?

[4]
cómo hablar si apenas te escuchamos cómo callar
si tu memoria adormece cómo dormir si tu lengua
nos devuelve a la ceniza

[5]
tanto hablas de ti que acabarás por ser otro dijo aburrida
la esfinge no la escucho difícil escuchar en el desierto te voy
a contar una historia un perro alado fue mi padre mi madre
una leona azul si lo prefieres una piedra un guijarro inmóvil
devorado por el viento escucha el viento su áspera música
enroscándose en mis alas cómo arden sus alas cómo aturden
mis ojos nublan para siempre mis orejas con qué ganas se ríe
con qué odio mastica pájaros escupe plumas a mis pies yo
las recojo las guardo en una caja doy de comer a mi caballo

[6]
un pie hundido en la espesura el otro atravesado de estrellas
así cantaba el ciego mira los campos de algodón el mar negro
surcado de trirremes de grullas acercándose a mi almohada
destruyendo las páginas del libro nunca pude terminar el libro
desplegar velas librarme para siempre del insomnio la noche
era oscura así cantaba el ciego en marlin en las plazas de grecia
en las calles malolientes y sucias de moscú ¿lo ves? dijo burlona
la esfinge a mí no puedes engañarme

of all the vegetable immodesty a heavenly scandal indeed the flowers
celebrate this wonder leaves fall to the ground turn dark colors
renounce the gods' supreme favor what have the dahlias
to say now?

[4]
how should you speak if we barely listen how should you keep silent
if your memory makes us drowse how should you sleep if your tongue
returns us to the ashes

[5]
you talk so much about yourself you'll end up being another person
the sphinx said bored i don't listen to her it's hard to hear in the
    desert
let me tell you a story my father was a winged dog my mother
a blue lioness or if you like a rock a motionless pebble
devoured by the wind listen to the wind its harsh music coiling
round my wings look how her wings burn how they dazzle
my eyes cloud my ears over forever how lustily she laughs
chewing up birds in sheer abhorrence spitting out feathers at my feet i
pick them up keep them in a box feed them to my horse

[6]
one foot in the thickets the other pierced with stars that's how
the blind man was singing look at the cottonfields the black sea
furrowed with triremes with cranes drawing close to my pillow
destroying the pages of the book i never managed to finish that
    book
unfurl sails or rid myself forever of insomnia the night was
dark that's what the blind man sang in marlin in greek plazas
in filthy foul-smelling moscow streets see him? the sphinx asked
mockingly me you can't fool me

[7]

si digo una palabra incendia la palabra si decido
callar pudre mi lengua si la miro a los ojos ordena
azul en arameo tira mis orejas hiere con la uña
la pureza del aire luego espera con qué paciencia
espera así mancho tus ojos dice así ensucio tu deseo

[8]

abre el cofre ordenó la esfinge verás niebla en su interior
palabras de otros estorbando el sueño no le dije veo
nieve copos diminutos que se encuentran y se unen
para apartarse después dónde has leído eso me pregunta
en un poema de lucrecio en su hoguera he ardido en sus
llamas he vuelto a nacer esta noche huele a amor huele
a flores muertas su recuerdo es ahora indestructible oh
sol de anteojos amarillos y despiadadas tijeras engáñame
una vez más oh sol de mirada impenetrable y lujuriosa
traciona mi deseo devuélveme el espejismo del amor
la palabra que duele la palabra que mata

[9]

el amor hiere los párpados enciende una antorcha
en cada dedo cría gusanos en los ojos esta noche no
hables de amor dijo la esfinge pensé que se burlaba
no he venido hasta aquí para escuchar no he venido
para ver lo tuyo es naufragar en el silencio respirar
con la mirada fue lo más amable que me dijo lo más
perturbador aquella noche tuve un sueño dos bueyes
araban en líneas paralelas primero una luego la otra
parecían trazar una sentencia dibujar un pentagrama
así forjamos el enigma me dijeron luego cayó nieve
y lo borró todo

[7]

if i utter a word she sets the word ablaze if i decide to keep
silent she makes my tongue rot if i look into her eyes she orders
blue in aramaic tugs on my ears wounds the air's purity
with her nails then waits how incredibly patiently she waits
this is how i'll blot out your eyes how i'll soil your desire

[8]

open the coffer the sphinx demanded you'll see mist inside
other people's words that keep you from sleeping no i said i see
snow tiny flakes coming together joining up with one another
only to separate later where did you read that she asked
in a poem by lucretius tied to his stake i've burnt in his
flames i am reborn tonight it smells like love it smells
like dead flowers her memory is indestructible now oh sun
sporting yellow eyeglasses sun wielding merciless scissors fool me
one more time oh you with that impenetrable lascivious gaze
betray my desire give me back the illusion of love
the word that hurts the word that kills

[9]

love wounds the eyelids lights a torch on every
finger raises worms in people's eyes tonight don't
talk about love the sphinx said i thought she was joking
i haven't come this far just to listen this far just
to see your fate is to capsize in silence to breathe through
your gaze that was the nicest thing she said to me the most
disturbing thing that night i had a dream two oxen were
plowing in parallel lines first one line then the other it looked
like they were writing out some maxim drawing a pentagram
that's how we create enigma they told me then the snow fell
and covered everything up

[10]

mis cartas de calor te llegan sin hacer ruido te gusta
ese verso sí dije de memoria son las aves que vuelan
por el roquerío que buscan peces muertos cadáveres
de focas y delfines no me dijo es la nieve que oprime
hasta sangrar tu lengua el hedor insoportable de la rosa
la hoguera donde arden aburridas las palabras ¿no es
mejor callar? sí le dije y me puse a escribir este poema

[10]
my heated letters arrive without fanfare you like
that line yes i recited by heart they are the birds that fly
along the rocks that look for dead fish the carcasses
of seals and dolphins no she said it's the snow that weighs down
your tongue until it bleeds the unbearable stench of the rose
the stake where bored words go up in flames isn't it better
to be quiet? yes i told her and started writing this poem

HUMO DE INCENDIOS LEJANOS

[1]
de dónde vendrá ese título humo de incendios lejanos
lo escuché en un parque en el dorso de una oreja rampante
y entregada la luna estaba roja el bosque como siempre pleno
de heliotropos y begonias azules lo escuché en un parque
un perro ladraba la luna estaba roja el sol ya se había ido

[2]
vigilaba mis pasos decía bien pero con menos énfasis
las palabras hedían cantaba con dulzura la serpiente
cuidado me dijo es un monstruo un animal deforme
hace años dejé sobre su espalda una hoja de tilo fue
sólo un rasguño una herida en la piel donde se graba
el tiempo donde duerme el halcón destrozado la sangre
en los pechos de krimilda recuerda la sangre en los
pechos de krimilda su muerte a manos de un cazador
de jabalíes la serpiente danzaba la luna estaba roja el
héroe no parecía darse cuenta he perdido la marmita
de oro dijo no sé quién me la ha robado

[3]
una vez los árboles se desprendieron de sus ramas
era primavera no soportaron el peso de la nieve
el sol lucía oscuro los ciervos bajaron de los montes
las ratas huyeron del pantano todo ante mí era alegoría
pero yo no escribí nada

THE SMOKE OF DISTANT FIRES

[1]
i wonder where the title the smoke of distant fires comes from
i heard it in a park once at the back of my creeping devoted
ear the moon was red the forest as always abloom with
heliotropes and blue begonias yes i heard it in a park once
a dog was barking the moon was red the sun had already set

[2]
eyeing my steps she'd say good but with less emphasis
the words stank to high heaven the serpent was singing sweetly
careful she told me it's a monstrosity a misshapen beast
years ago i placed a leaf from a linden tree on his back
which left only a scratch a mere flesh wound where time
records its march where the mangled falcon sleeps the blood
on kriemhild's breasts recalling the blood on kriemhild's
breasts her death at the hands of some hunter of wild
boars the serpent was dancing the moon was red the
hero didn't seem to notice i have lost the pot of gold
he said i don't know who could have stolen it from me

[3]
the trees let go of their branches allowing them to fall
it was spring and they couldn't bear the weight of the snow
the sun shone darkly deer came down from the hills
rats fled the swamp and everything before me was allegory
yet i didn't write a word

[4]

¿quién vigila mis pasos? ¿quién me dicta sus palabras?
¿quién me dice ahora es el momento? no sé

quién vigila mis pasos quién me dicta sus palabras quién
me dice ahora es el momento

[5]

estoy con mis padres en melbourne debe ser un sueño
nunca he estado en melbourne mis padres miran con
indiferencia el plato de comida me siento incómodo
en momentos así te recuerdo nunca voy más allá de
tus ojos no tengo ojos pregúntale a sigfrido a la serpiente
pregúntale qué fue de tus palabras de los papeles que
arrojaste al canasto de la esperada lluvia en un bosque
de tilos hablo del infierno de la moneda de caronte
del perro que ladra del perro que no nos deja dormir

[6]

no estamos en melbourne no estamos en un sueño
en verdad no sé dónde estamos hay un parque escucho
una música un rumor de hojas esta noche estamos solos
pareces un tigre amo tu miedo la veta de luz que desgarra
tu sombra el manto solar donde arde la belleza olvida un
momento la piel olvida un momento la belleza esta noche
estás conmigo me pregunta por qué la luna está tan roja

[7]

no es de noche no estamos en un parque estamos en tebaida
es el comienzo o el final de una tormenta es como un verso
que sabes de memoria es tan dura la memoria ella conserva
una columna de mármol un desierto rojo y nada alrededor

[4]
who is eyeing my steps? who is dictating me words?
who is telling me now is the time? i don't know

who is eyeing my steps who is dictating me words who
is telling me now is the time

[5]
i'm with my parents in melbourne this has to be a dream
i've never been to melbourne my parents look at a plate of
food with no interest one way or the other i feel uncomfortable
at times that's how i remember you i can never get past
your eyes i don't have any eyes ask siegfried ask the serpent
ask him what's become of your words of the papers you
tossed in the wastebasket of the much hoped-for rain in the linden
tree forest i'm talking about hell about charon's coins
about the barking dog the one that won't let us sleep

[6]
we're not in melbourne and this is no dream truth
to tell i don't know where we are i see a park nearby hear
some music the rustling of leaves we're alone tonight
you're like a tiger i love your fear the streak of light rending
your shadow the solar mantle where beauty burns forget
the flesh for a moment forget about beauty for now you're
with me tonight why is the moon so red she asks

[7]
it isn't night and we aren't in a park we're in thebais
at either the beginning or the end of a storm it's like a line
you know by heart memory can be so cruel preserving
a marble column a red desert and nothing else around them

sólo piedras arañas alacranes una multitud piadosa y un conejo
me pregunta por qué una multitud piadosa por qué un conejo
lo habré visto en un poema en un cuadro medieval tal vez
en un cortometraje yo oraba en lo alto detenía la serpiente
si una nube rozaba mis orejas agradecía a dios era su mano
me ordenaba leer a mí nadie me enseñó a leer

[8]
entonces debes ser simón me dijo señalando mis sandalias
mi torpeza mis ojos llenos de desierto

[9]
escucha el rumor de las hojas escucha el silbido del viento
dime que siempre estuvimos aquí dime que nunca te fuiste
léeme en voz alta la traición del héroe el sueño del águila
devorándose al halcón dime que es de noche los vecinos
saludan con indiferencia las aves desarman sus nidos
en la orilla un perro ladra un perro no nos deja dormir

[10]
lugar común agua y barro dibujan su alfabeto la metáfora
arde la veo consumirse en los despojos no es necesario
escribir no es necesario leer esta noche la serpiente
está muy excitada celebra un nacimiento las palabras
se pudren la luna brilla en la palma de caronte ¿qué hacer?

consérvala me dice escribe humo de incendios lejanos

but rocks spiders scorpions a pious crowd and a rabbit
why a pious crowd she asks why a rabbit i must have read
about them in a poem seen them in a medieval painting or some
movie short perhaps praying high in the air i grasped the serpent
and if a cloud brushed my ears i gave god thanks for it was his hand
he ordered me to read but no one had ever taught me how

[8]
you must be simeon then she said pointing out my sandals
my lack of social graces my eyes brimming over with desert

[9]
she listens to the rustling of the leaves to the whistling of the wind
tell me we've always been here tell me you never went away
read me the part about the hero's betrayal the dream of the eagle
devouring the falcon tell me it's nighttime our neighbors wave
at us with no interest one way or the other the birds pick apart
    their nests
on the riverbank a dog barks a dog that won't let us sleep

[10]
water and mud common ground sketch their alphabet the metaphor
is burning i see it shrivel to nothing amid the rubble we don't
need to write don't need to read tonight the serpent
is very excited for it's celebrating a birth as the words rot
and the moon shines on charon's palm what should i do?

hold on to it she says write the smoke of distant fires

NOTES

"Love Poem with Dark Face"

The epigraph from "Vrai nom" (Real name) in *Du mouvement et de l'immobilité de Douve* (On the Motion and Immobility of Douve)— Paris: Mercure de France, 1953, p. 41—may be translated as "I will hold in my hands your dark face."

•

"A Theory of Sight After a Poem by Seferis"

The epigraph is the title of George Seferis's poem "Summer Solstice" followed by the number "11" designating the section from which the references strewn throughout "A Theory of Sight After a Poem by Seferis" appear. The translation from the Greek, by Edmund Keeley and Philip Sherrard, was published in *George Seferis: Collected Poems*. Princeton: Princeton University Press, 1995, pp. 206-14.

"Notes for a Confession with Rutabagas"

The epigraph is from "Farm Implements and Rutabagas in a Landscape" in *The Double Dream of Spring*. New York: E. P. Dutton & Co., Inc., 1970, pp. 47-48.

The dialogue from the comic strip of January 17, 1929, by Elzie Crisler Segar, is from the *Thimble Theater* series published in the *New York Journal,* which introduced the character of Popeye the Sailor later popularized by Max Fleischer.

•

"The Book of My Life or My Conversations with Saint Teresa of Ávila"

The epigraph is from *The Life of Saint Teresa of Ávila by Herself,"* translated by J. M. Cohen. London: Penguin Books, 1957, p. 221. The poem makes references to incidents that appear in the autobiography.

•

"Fable of the Lark and the Moon"

The first epigraph, the opening lines of "Die Achte Elegie," translated as "The Eighth Elegy" by Edward Snow, reads: "With all its eyes the animal world / beholds the Open." In *Duino Elegies*. New York: North Point Press, 2000, p. 47.

The second epigraph from "Dym" (Smoke) in *Pragnienie* (Desire)— Cracow: Wydawnictwo, 2000, p. 46—may be translated as "the full moon enters our houses."

"Athanasius and the Ark or the Conversion of Saint Eustace"

The epigraph, in G. J. Racz's translation, is from *Arca Noë*, Book I, Section iii, Chapter 4.

•

"Putting My Library in Order Before Bedtime"

The epigraph from "Linişte," translated as "Silence" by Brenda Walker and Stelian Apostolescu, reads: "In my breast / a strange voice has woken / and a song of longing sings in me—a longing/ that's not mine." In *Complete Poetical Works of Lucian Blaga, 1895-1961*. Iaşi, Oxford, Portland: The Center for Romanian Studies, 2001, p. 60. The last line in Stanza 9 uses a variant from this translation.

•

"Thirteen Winters with Snow"

The epigraph is from "Desert Places" in *The Poetry of Robert Frost: The Collected Poems, Complete and Unabridged*, ed. Edward Connery Lathem. New York: Henry Holt and Company, 1969, p. 296.

•

"Exercises for Blocking Out the Rain"

The epigraph is from "Poem 177 (449)" in *Final Harvest: Emily Dickinson's Poems*, ed. Thomas H. Johnson. Boston and Toronto: Little, Brown and Company, 1961, p. 107.

"What the Birdsong Says"

The epigraph from "Piccolo Testamento," translated as "Little Testament" by Cid Corman, reads: "but a history endures in ashes alone / and persistence is only extinction." In *Eugenio Montale: Selected Poems*. New York: New Directions, 1965, p. 161.

•

"Letters that Arrive without Fanfare"

The first epigraph from "Poem 78," translated by Clarence Brown and W. S. Merwin, reads: "Insomnia. Homer. Taut sails." In *Osip Mandelstam: Selected Poems*. New York: Atheneum, 1974, p. 8.

The second epigraph from "Rivage où commencent les conjectures" (Shore where conjectures begin) in *Versión celeste* (Barcelona: Barral Editores, 1970, p. 110), may be translated as "Your heated letters arrive without fanfare."

Eduardo Chirinos, an internationally acclaimed voice of Latin American letters, is professor of Modern and Classical Languages and Literatures at the University of Montana. A member of Peru's '80s Generation, which came of age after a decade of military dictatorship, Chirinos won the Premio Casa de América in 2001 for his volume *Breve historia de la música* (A Brief History of Music) and the Premio Generación del 27 in 2009 for *Mientras el lobo está* (While the Wolf Is Around).

G. J. Racz is associate professor of Foreign Languages and Literature at Long Island University–Brooklyn, president of the American Literary Translators Association, and review editor for *Translation Review*.

Daniel Shapiro is a poet and translator whose work has appeared in *The American Poetry Review*, *BOMB*, *The Brooklyn Rail*, and *The Quarterly Conversation*. His translation of Tomás Harris's *Cipango* was published by Bucknell University Press. He is Director of Literature and Editor of *Review* at the Americas Society in New York.

Open Letter—the University of Rochester's nonprofit, literary translation press—is one of only a handful of publishing houses dedicated to increasing access to world literature for English readers. Publishing ten titles in translation each year, Open Letter searches for works that are extraordinary and influential, works that we hope will become the classics of tomorrow.

Making world literature available in English is crucial to opening our cultural borders, and its availability plays a vital role in maintaining a healthy and vibrant book culture. Open Letter strives to cultivate an audience for these works by helping readers discover imaginative, stunning works of fiction and by creating a constellation of international writing that is engaging, stimulating, and enduring.

Current and forthcoming titles from Open Letter include works from Argentina, Bulgaria, Catalonia, China, Poland, Serbia, and many other countries.

www.openletterbooks.org